VEGAN
RECIPES FROM
INDIA

To all the women who don't wear a chef's hat or have stars, but who feed and delight us every single day.

VEGAN RECIPES FROM INDIA

— ભારતી વેઘાન રસોઈ —

Recipes from a Gujarati family

NATASHA &
YASMINE TOURABI

Photographs by Manon Gouhier

GRUB STREET • LONDON

Contents

Preface

This book was born out of my own personal desire to set down the Indian recipes that nourished me since I was a child.

As the daughter of a migrant family from the western Indian state of Gujarat, cooking is the deepest and most precious link I have with my Indian culture. It was at the table, enjoying a glass of chai along with a snack of vegetable pakoras, a biryani for special occasions or a glass of saffron- and cardamom-scented hot milk in winter, that I was introduced not only to the flavours of Gujarat, but also to the rituals, symbols and knowledge of our culture.

My maternal grandparents were born and raised in Gujarat before moving to Mumbai, which is in Maharashtra. Shortly after my mother was born, they left for Madagascar, where they lived for almost 25 years before settling in the Rhône-Alpes region of France in the 1970s.

My mother returned to India for a few years, specifically to Udaipur in Rajasthan, where she lived until the last months of her first pregnancy, before returning to Grenoble where I was born. Despite crossing so many borders and spending decades away from Gujarat and India, our family recipes have continued to be passed down from generation to generation, enriched by the flavours and ingredients of the lands they have traversed.

Now that my grandmother is no longer with us, my aunt is over 85 and mother is almost 75, I feel a duty to ensure that their culinary and cultural knowledge is preserved and passed on. Unlike them, I didn't spend enough hours in the kitchen with my mother, so didn't fully master the basics of these recipes, which I love as much as they delight me. It wasn't until I was an adult – geographically far away from my family, unable to relish their good food and my strongest link with India – that I felt the need to learn for myself how to make the dishes I've always enjoyed, but without any animal products. Although I went vegan about ten years ago, over time I've learnt to veganise each and every recipe to faithfully recapture the textures and flavours of my favourite dishes. As my family is particularly open-minded, curious and creative when it comes to cooking, they loved the idea of accompanying me on this culinary adventure.

In addition to this very personal reason, my mother and I wish to offer you an authentic introduction to the flavours and dishes of Gujarat and beyond. As Indian cuisine is so often appropriated and adapted in the West, few people are lucky enough to appreciate its diversity and understand what makes it so special. We hope that the recipes and know-how shared here will allow you to discover the wealth and uniqueness of each regional Indian cuisine.

As well as recipes for *shaak* (vegetable-based dishes), dal (pulse-based dishes), rice, flatbreads, condiments, *mithai* (sweets) and drinks, as you go along you'll find specific tips on each technique and ingredient to help you understand how and why they are used.

Over the past few years, my mother and I spent many, many hours together in the kitchen working on this collaborative project, and, while she taught me the culinary basics I lacked, I introduced her to plant-based alternatives. And so, together, we tested and tasted, analysed, remade and improved each of the recipes in this book.

My job was to scrupulously weigh each ingredient, meticulously jot down every detail and to write the text of the book. It was then proofread by my mother, who mindfully added the finishing touches, including her discreet advice, so that you can reproduce the flavours, aromas and textures of our cuisine in your own home.

I hope that you enjoy discovering these delicious recipes that my mother, my aunt Banou and my cousins Zehra and Ilmasse, have faithfully passed on to me with patience and love.

Natasha

Introduction

Indian cuisine

Indian cuisine, plural cuisines

In a country that covers more than 3 million square kilometres, is made up of 28 states and eight Union Territories, where over 230 languages and several thousand dialects are spoken, it is unsurprising to find cultures – and therefore cuisines – that are very different from one region to another, each influenced by its own colonial history, climate and geographical location. While the cuisines of northern India are steeped in Mughal influences, that of Goa, on the south-west coast, has retained traces of the Portuguese presence there, and dishes from the north-east of India have incorporated ingredients and techniques from neighbouring South-East Asian countries. Although similar types of dishes can be found throughout the country – meat or vegetables in a sauce, dal, dishes made with rice, all kinds of fried foods, pickles, chutneys, flatbreads, etc. – the ingredients used and preparation techniques are markedly, if not radically, different from one region to another.

Let's look at *roti* as an example: These flatbreads are usually made from wholegrain wheat flour (*atta*) in northern India and are known as tandoori *rotis*; made with yoghurt, they are then baked in a tandoor oven. However, in Rajasthan they make *bajra rotis* with wholegrain millet flour, while in Karnataka their version, called *jowar rotis*, are made with sorghum flour. Furthermore, some specialities specific to one region have no equivalent elsewhere, such as the *dosas* of Southern India – very thin pancakes prepared with a fermented batter made with rice and pulse flours. Last but not least, the availability of certain products and ingredients also has a considerable influence on Indian cuisine. For instance, coconut is used in various forms in Southern India, but is less commonly encountered in the north, where dairy products play a more important role.

Although there are specialities common to the whole of India, the traditional composition of everyday meals – like that of festive meals – varies greatly from one region to another. For example, what is served up on a family's table in a coastal village in Kerala will be very different from that of a village high in the mountainous region of Ladakh. As for the western state of Gujarat, despite its 1,600 kilometres of coastline, it is better known for its vegetarian cuisine than for its fish and seafood dishes. In fact, it is home to a wide range of recipes: pan-fried dishes and sauced ones, stuffed vegetables, countless dals, as well as cereal- and pulse-based snacks. *Kitchri* (lentils and rice), *bajra na rotla* (wholegrain millet flour flatbreads), mango juice and *tchaas* (a spiced, salted yoghurt drink) are among the most beloved foods and drinks in this region, while *dhokla* (spongy cakes made from fermented flour), *doodh pak* (a kind of rice pudding) and *shrikhand* (spiced strained yoghurt) are among the best-known Gujarati dishes across the country.

The place of vegetarianism and veganism

Did you know that India holds two world records? The highest percentage of vegetarians (around 25% of the population[1] compared with 8% that identify as vegetarians in the UK[2]) and the lowest meat consumption (3.78 kg per year per inhabitant compared with around 79.9 kg in the UK[3]). Many people who eat little or no meat do so on religious grounds. The principal vow of *ahimsa* – meaning non-violence – taken by Jains, entails eating no animal flesh, honey or eggs. *Ahimsa*, which

1 Not least because of the taboo that can surround the consumption of meat, exact figures are difficult to obtain and vary from 20% to 40%.
2 https://en.wikipedia.org/wiki/Vegetarianism_by_country
3 https://en.wikipedia.org/wiki/List_of_countries_by_meat_consumption

encompasses compassion and respect for all living creatures, is also one of the tenets of Hinduism, in which vegetarianism is advocated in certain texts. This is why only 44%[4] of Hindus are vegetarians, bearing in mind that most Hindus avoid beef because of the sacred nature of the cow, and refrain from eating meat during particular religious celebrations. Although meat is not banned in Sikhism and Buddhism, some communities, also influenced by the principle of non-violence enshrined in these two religions, refrain from eating it.

In fact, Indian cuisines – from every region – give pride of place to vegetarian dishes. What's more, if you replace ghee (clarified butter), which is commonly used to fry spices in or brush over flatbreads, it's also easy to enjoy a varied, balanced vegan diet in a country where myriad vegetables, cereals and pulses are both grown and cooked.

Indian-style eating

Having been born and brought up in France, I was immersed in two very different culinary cultures, but it wasn't until I met my husband, who is from Poitou, that I realised how much my eating habits were influenced by my Indian background, in which meals generally consist of a main course with various side dishes and condiments that are served all together. This is the principle behind *thali*: a stainless-steel platter with several compartments or bowls in which some ten different dishes are served in small portions – rice, flatbreads, one or more *shaak*, a dal, crudités, chutneys, pickles, a dessert and a drink – that results in a meal of myriad flavours and textures.

In my husband's family, meals are divided into four very distinct stages: starter, main course, cheese platter and salad, and a dessert at the end. Conversely, in my family we don't usually end our daily meals on a sweet note, as sweets such as *mithai* are eaten at the start of a meal and generally only on festive occasions and during religious celebrations. As for cheese, generous platters are also reserved for special occasions. Although I of course ate and enjoyed structured 'French-style' meals throughout my childhood – at the school canteen or at the home of friends, and even sometimes with my own family – this is not the norm for me.

Among other notable differences concerning meals, I've noticed that, in a society where children are taught to eat with cutlery, those who eat with their hands are often subject to racist and/or dehumanising slurs, which are particularly hurtful for those of us to whom it is natural to eat in this way. However, I have never given up that unique pleasure that imbues our meals with a very special flavour and feel.

I invite you to take pleasure in these recipes in your own way, adapting them to your personal eating habits and traditions, but I would like to point out that the dishes that make up Indian cooking are an integral part of a culture where meals are composed and eaten differently. In fact, every cuisine is so much more than just the ingredients, combinations and techniques that define it, and each meal is also shaped by the customs and beliefs associated with it.

4 https://www.pewresearch.org/short-reads/2021/07/08/eight-in-ten-indians-limit-meat-in-their-diets-and-four-in-ten-consider-themselves-vegetarian/

Basic ingredients

Preparing dishes from distant lands usually involves discovering all sorts of ingredients, and that can seem rather intimidating at first. But fear not, most of the ingredients used in these recipes are readily available in supermarkets or shops selling organic products, and some of the ingredients are even produced in this country. More importantly, in an effort to be environmentally friendly and to cater to different tastes, we mainly cook with locally grown fruit and vegetables, adapting our menus according to the season and the produce available at local markets. When it comes to other ingredients, there are a number of specialist brick-and-mortar establishments and online shops where you can buy more unusual products.

SPICES

Asafoetida

Asafoetida is a gum resin extracted from a specific rhizome or taproot. Its hard, gum-like texture and semi-precious stone appearance in shades of pink or brown are as surprising as its smell, which is similar to that of rotten eggs! But once it has sizzled in hot oil the smell disappears, giving way to much more pleasant aromas of garlic and onion. Renowned for its digestive properties, we generally put a pinch of it in a *vaghar* when making dal, but its use is optional in all our recipes. Personally, I prefer to use it whole, grating it as required, rather than ground, as the latter has usually been mixed with flour (regular or gluten-free) to make it easier to use.

Bay leaves, Indian

Different from the European bay variety (*Laurus nobilis*), Indian bay leaves (*Cinnamomum tamala*) have broader, longer, darker and smoother leaves, and with three veins rather than a single central one. Appreciated for their cinnamon-like flavour, we add them mainly to our rice-based dishes. You will usually find them under the Hindi name *tej patta*.

Black pepper

A spice commonly used in Europe, black pepper comes from a tropical climbing plant native to Southern India. After being harvested, the peppercorns are blanched then dried to preserve them and intensify their floral, fruity and woody aromas. Added whole to a *vaghar*, they give a pleasant spiciness to rice dishes, without making them piquant. Remember to remove the peppercorns before serving your dish to avoid anyone chewing them!

Black salt

This condiment, called *kala namak* in India (literally 'black salt'), is used not only to salt dishes, but also to give them a sulphur-like flavour reminiscent of eggs. We add a few pinches to scrambled tofu as well as to *masala tchaas*.

Cardamom, green

The dried fruit of a herbaceous plant of the same name, green cardamom can be used whole or ground, with or without the pod. Its floral, herbaceous and mentholated aroma is concentrated in the seeds, so it's best to crush and split the pods or put the seeds directly into hot oil. However, be careful as not everyone likes to bite down on them! As a general rule, we use whole, split and crushed pods in our savoury dishes and ground cardamom for our desserts. An exception is flan, as the seeds can easily be strained.

Cardamom, black

Despite their similar shape and name, black cardamom is very different from green cardamom. Black cardamom has much bigger pods, and its smoky, camphor-like aroma is obtained from being dried directly over a naked flame. Its very strong fragrance means its use is limited to savoury dishes, and it is particularly popular as a flavouring for rice.

Chilli peppers

Chillies are found in almost every dish, fresh or dried, whole or chopped, powdered or in flakes. Of the many varieties of chilli used in India, the Kashmiri and Jwala are among the most common. The former, with a sweet, fruity flavour, is generally a bright red, not very pungent powder with a score of 1,500–2,000 on the Scoville scale (named after the pharmacologist who invented a scale for measuring the heat of chillies). The latter, whose name means 'flame' in Sanskrit, is much stronger (30,000–50,000 on the Scoville scale) and tends to be used raw. Contrary to popular belief, not all chilli peppers are hot. It depends on the variety and what form they take: for instance, one dried chilli contains more capsaicin and can be as hot as two fresh chillies. It is also important to know that the molecules responsible for the heat of a chilli are mainly found in the white membranes surrounding and holding the seeds. Therefore, the pungency of a chilli can be reduced if you remove these parts and use only the flesh.

In the recipes in this book, we usually state that chillies are optional. Whether or not you use chillies for these dishes, and how much and what form they take, is up to you. However, we often use both finely chopped fresh chillies and chilli powder in the same recipe. The former is added at the same time as the garlic and ginger pastes, while the latter is added to the pan along with the ground spices. If you don't want even the slightest hint of heat, we recommend using red bell peppers, Anaheim chillies or sweet paprika powder. For a slightly more piquant dish, go for Espelette chillies, poblano chillies or Kashmiri chilli powder. For a much hotter dish, use jalapeño and serrano peppers. And, last but not least, if you're fine with a scorchingly fiery sensation in your mouth, you'll most likely love cayenne, bird's eye or habanero chillies. Remember that different chillies have different flavours, so some varieties – such as those listed here – are better suited to Indian cuisine than others.

Cinnamon

We use two varieties of cinnamon in our recipes: **Ceylon cinnamon** and **cassia bark**, of which different varieties are grown in China, Indonesia, India and Vietnam. The former, appreciated for its subtle notes of wood and caramel, comes in the form of rolls – called quills – of fairly thin, light-coloured bark. The latter, which is less expensive and much stronger in flavour, is generally in the form of darker sticks or small pieces. We tend to use cassia bark for *chai*, as well as in our everyday dishes like *shaaks*, dals and spiced rice, but like to add Ceylon cinnamon to our festive rice dishes such as *biryanis*.

Handle chillies with care

Chillies don't just burn your mouth; they can also irritate mucous membranes and your airways. Here are a few important tips to help you avoid unpleasant incidents when handling chillies:

- Before grinding dried chillies into powder, protect your eyes and airways. Go outdoors to open your spice mill and to transfer the powder to an airtight container. Even the slightest residue of chilli powder in the air can seriously irritate your airways.
- Before cutting a fresh chilli pepper, put on vinyl or latex gloves to prevent your skin from coming into contact with the seeds and membranes.

Cloves

A warm spice with a powerful aroma, cloves are the flower buds of the clove tree, a plant native to Indonesia, but which today is also grown in India, Sri Lanka, Pakistan, Madagascar and Tanzania. We prefer whole cloves for flavouring our dals and rice, as well as in our recipes for garam masala and tandoori paste.

Coriander

There are very few recipes in which we don't use either whole or ground coriander, and we use the fresh leaves as well. Now cultivated all over the world, locally grown coriander seeds are easy to find. Although citrusy notes are a feature of all varieties, coriander grown in India tends to be sweeter and lighter than its European counterpart, which is more lemony and herbaceous. We use both whole and ground coriander in our recipes.

Cumin

Found in most of our recipes, and often combined with coriander, cumin's floral notes soften its bitterness. Its full potential is usually revealed when the seeds are toasted and then ground (see p. 158 for recipe), but even untoasted, it still adds a lovely woody, earthy aroma to all kinds of dishes.

Curry leaves

These leaves of the *Murraya koenigii* tree, native to India, are used to flavour all kinds of dishes throughout South and South-East Asia. Fresh curry leaves have a somewhat citrusy aroma with floral and musky notes, enhancing all kinds of *shaak* and dal dishes. Dried curry leaves tend to have little flavour, so I recommend buying them fresh and freezing them after washing and drying them thoroughly. Rarely available in non-specialised shops, you can buy them in brick-and-mortar establishments and online shops specialising in spices.

Fenugreek

A herbaceous plant native to North Africa, fenugreek is a spice whose seeds and leaves – both fresh and dried – are used. Renowned for their digestive properties, fenugreek seeds (*methi*) have a nutty flavour, and are usually added to a *vaghar* when making dal. As fresh leaves are hard to come by here, we use crushed dried leaves (*kasoori methi*): their earthy notes add depth and complexity to various sauced dishes, and they are also used to season flatbreads such as *parathas*.

Garam masala

Garam masala is a blend of spices renowned for its warming properties. It is composed of aromatic molecules found in hot phenols (cinnamon, cloves and star anise), earthy terpenes (nutmeg and cumin) and penetrating terpenes (green and black cardamom and bay leaves). The word garam masala is made up of the words 'hot' (*garam*) and 'spices' (*masala*). As every family has its own recipe, the composition and flavour of garam masala can vary from household to household (or from brand to brand), but it is generally added at the end of the cooking process to enhance the flavour of a dish. I invite you to discover my recipe on p. 161.

Mustard seeds, black

Of the three main varieties of mustard – black (*Brassica nigra*), yellow (*Brassica juncea*) and white (*Brassica alba*) – black mustard is the most widespread in India. When added to hot oil, these seeds release subtle peppery aromas with bitter nuances that are much appreciated in all kinds of pickles, salads and *shaak* vegetable dishes. These little black seeds have a tendency to shoot out when you fry them in oil, so be sure to cover the pan when preparing your *vaghar*.

Nutmeg

The nutmeg tree, native to Indonesia, is unique as it produces two distinct spices: nutmeg, which is simply the seed, and mace, the fibrous lacy aril that surrounds it. Although both are used in Indian cuisine, this book only calls for nutmeg. It should be grated as needed, as nutmeg's essential oils are highly volatile.

Saffron

These particularly delicate bright red strands are simply the stigmas of the crocus flower. Hand-picked in autumn, just before sunrise, the harvesting and drying processes are particularly demanding, which explains the high price of saffron. Fortunately, and as long as you buy quality saffron and prepare it properly, only a little is needed to enjoy its unique, warm musky flavour. Choose saffron strands rather than powder and make sure they are completely dry – they should be quite brittle and break easily. If not, toast them in a dry pan for a few seconds. Crush the desired number of saffron strands and infuse them in a little hot water for between 1 and 24 hours before adding the resulting yellow liquid to your dish. It is best to add the saffron-infused water at the end of the cooking process to preserve the intensity of the flavour and avoid any bitterness developing.

Star anise

The fruit of a shrub native to south-west China and north-east Vietnam, star anise (one of the ingredients in the Chinese 'five spice' mix) is grown in several Asian countries. Its sweet aroma, reminiscent of liquorice and fennel, is concentrated mainly in its carpels – the 'petals' containing the seeds – and wonderfully enhances *biryanis* as well as garam masala, and even a good *masala chai*.

Turmeric

A spice obtained from rhizomes that are dried and then ground, turmeric is easily recognised by its yellow-orange hue, which not only adds colour but also peppery, lemony and floral notes to dishes. This is a spice whose flavour and pungency varies considerably from one brand to another.

Vanilla

Native to Mexico and Central America, vanilla is the fruit of a tropical orchid and comes in the form of fleshy black pods. To make the most of its aroma, split the pod in half and scrape out the seeds with the tip of a knife, then add the seeds and the pods to your dish. Don't forget to remove the pods before serving.

How to best store spices

As spices are sensitive to humidity, heat and light, we recommend that you:

- Choose spices that come in opaque sachets or jars;
- Store in opaque, airtight containers;
- Store in a cool, dry place away from all sources of heat.

Despite having a shelf life of several years, the fragrance of a spice will fade over a period of months. So, as well as following the advice above, it's also best to:

- Buy/grind spices in small quantities according to your needs;
- Store ground spices for 6 months to 1 year;
- Store whole spices for 1 to 2 years.

These time frames are, of course, just a guide. For example, spices stored in optimal conditions will retain their flavour for longer than those stored in transparent jars above a hob, which will lose their fragrance after a few weeks. The best way to find out whether your spices still have their full flavour is to use your senses. For instance, if a spice is dull in colour, tastes and smells bland, and/or has a lumpy or damp texture, it is no longer fit for use.

Grind your own spices

Although you can find some excellent shop-bought ground spices, grinding your own using a mortar, electric or manual spice mill, or other means is a good idea in terms of both taste and cost.

A mortar and pestle

A mortar is particularly suitable for grinding small quantities, such as a couple of spoonfuls, of spices. A very versatile tool that can also be used to crush herbs, garlic, ginger and chillies, etc. Of the various materials available, we recommend choosing a model made of granite or stone. These materials are very robust, unlike porcelain and ceramic, and are non-porous, unlike wood. They also do not react with acidic ingredients, as marble and metal do.

An electric spice mill

Requiring much less effort, it results in a coarse or fine powder depending on your needs, and lets you grind large quantities of spices very quickly.

Manual spice mills

In addition to traditional pepper mills, there are other manual mills designed for grinding specific spices, such as dried chillies, nutmeg and even cinnamon. Remember that these mills should only be used for spices that are used regularly at home, such as pepper.

Other means

If you don't have any tools designed specifically for grinding spices, you can use what you already have on hand:

- **A fine grater**, such as a Microplane®, for grating larger, hard spices like cinnamon, nutmeg, star anise and black cardamom. This type of grater is also very handy for making fresh ginger or garlic paste (see p. 152 for recipes).
- **A plastic food bag and a kitchen mallet.** Simply place your spices in the bag, close it and place it on a solid surface, such as a chopping board, then pound repeatedly with a kitchen mallet to the desired consistency.
- **An electric coffee grinder.** As long as you can wash it, it can grind your spices to a powder – just make sure you don't end up with coffee mixed with spices or spices mixed with coffee!

PULSES

Pulses are an important source of plant-based protein in India. We eat around fifteen different varieties in the form of dals, fritters or flours. As it is impossible to offer as many recipes as there are pulses, we hope that the few varieties we have chosen will offer a glimpse of how diverse they are.

Chana dal

Chana dal is an Indian variety of hulled, split black chickpea, smaller and firmer than yellow chickpeas, and which you can enjoy in two of our recipes: an aubergine and pepper *shaak* and a dal.

Recommended soaking time: 12–24 hours.

Butter beans

White in colour and particularly creamy, butter beans are a large variety of lima bean. They can be replaced by cannellini beans, that are just as tender. We usually cook them as a dal, whole or blended.

Recommended soaking time: 12–24 hours.

Mung beans

Also known as green soya beans, mung beans come in three different forms: whole (mung beans), broken (mung dal *chilka*) or hulled and split (mung dal). We use whole, sprouted mung beans in a *shaak*, and hulled and split ones in our fritter, samosa and rice with lentils recipes.

Recommended soaking time: 12–24 hours for whole mung beans, 6–12 hours for split mung beans and 4–6 hours for hulled and split mung beans.

Masoor dal

Whole *masoor* dal are brown lentils, but when hulled they are a lovely coral colour. We use the former in the recipes for *masoor* dal and rice with lentils and vegetables (*poulao*) and the latter in our Four-pulse dal.

Recommended soaking time: 6–12 hours for whole masoor dal and 1–4 hours for hulled masoor dal.

Toor dal

A yellow, hulled split pea, *toor* dal is similar to the green split peas that are common in European kitchens. Like red, split lentils, this variety of pulse has a very melt-in-the-mouth texture when cooked. It is also an ingredient in our Four-pulse dal.

Recommended soaking time: 4–6 hours.

Tips for preparing pulses

If you're not used to cooking pulses, here are a few tips to make them easier to cook and also to digest.

- Rinse the pulses 2 or 3 times in cold water, until the water runs clear.
- Soak them to optimise nutrient absorption and make them easier to digest. This will also help to reduce the cooking time.
- Change the soaking water after 12 hours if they are left to soak for longer.
- Add ½ teaspoon of bicarbonate of soda to the soaking water for every 500 g of pulses (dry weight). This will soften their skins, making them easier to digest.

FLOURS

Atta flour

A stone-ground Indian durum flour, finer and lighter than other wholegrain flours. It results in a very pliable dough that is easy to roll out for flatbreads such as chapatis, puris and parathas. *Atta* flour, which is difficult to find outside of grocery shops specialising in South Asian products, can be substituted by a more locally available stone-ground durum wheat flour. However, as the wheat varieties used in India differ from those used in Europe, the result is likely to be significantly different. In any case, I would advise against substituting *atta* flour with soft wheat flour or industrially milled flour, as you'll find it difficult to make a dough and it will be hard to make the soft, fluffy breads in this book.

T45 flour

White T45 wheat flour is used to make puffed-up naans, but also to make thin, firm sheets of samosa dough. You can substitute it with T55 wheat flour, but as this is less easy to work with and contains less gluten, the result will be quite different.

Chickpea flour

In India, chickpea flour is used to make all kinds of flatbreads, fritters and other fried foods. Called *gram* or *besan* flour, it is made from *chana* dal. The taste is slightly different from European chickpea flour made from yellow chickpeas, but it is a perfectly acceptable substitute.

Brown rice flour

We use wholegrain rice flour to make *firni*, and also add it our doughnut batter for a crispier result. You will get equally good results using semi-wholegrain rice flour.

BASMATI RICE

With its long, white grains and floral aroma, basmati is undoubtedly the best-known variety of Indian rice in the world, and it's also the one we eat every day at home. To obtain delicious fluffy grains of rice that are not sticky, our tips are to:

- rinse the rice 3–4 times in cold water, until the water runs clear – this will remove much of the starch;

- leave the rice to soak for 20–30 minutes after rinsing – the cooking time will be shorter and the grains will be plumper and more flavoursome;

- cook the rice in a saucepan big enough so that the grains have enough room to swell properly and cook evenly;

- release as much steam as possible after cooking by carefully lifting and fluffing the rice with a wide spatula or rice spoon, taking care not to crush it.

PLANT-BASED ALTERNATIVES

None of the following ingredients or products are traditional Indian ingredients, but we have used them to substitute meat, eggs and dairy produce in our recipes.

Tofu

Made from yellow soya beans, tofu is a food traditionally used in several regions of East and South-East Asia. Of the many varieties of tofu available, we only use two in this book: plain firm tofu and silken tofu. The former can be used in place of chicken in our recipes for coriander tofu, cumin tofu and tandoori tofu and, combined with silken tofu, it can be used instead of eggs in our spiced scrambled tofu dish. As not all commercial tofus are the same, it is best to use fresh tofu rather than the long-life variety.

Plant-based milks

As long as you choose the right one, plant-based milk is a great substitute for cow's milk in our recipes. While soya milk can be used to make our delicious silky carrots with vanilla, give lovely flan-like textures and be used in our creamy rice pudding, we prefer other 'full-fat', 'creamy' or 'silky' plant-based milks for using in spiced milky tea and regular rice pudding. Enriched with fat, these milks are generally made from oats or a mixture of oats and soya beans. We particularly like, and so recommend, the following brands: Oatly® and Alpro®.

Soya yoghurt

Soya yoghurt can be used instead of regular milk yoghurt in some of our savoury and sweet recipes, such as *biryani,* grilled aubergine mash and *lassi*. We do not recommend using any other type of plant-based yoghurt as their texture and taste may not be suitable for our recipes.

Soya cream

Soya cream is called for in some of our sweets. Although we prefer it to other plant-based creams because of its neutral taste, you can replace it with any other plant-based cream of your choice.

Plant-based margarine

We use plant-based margarine instead of ghee (clarified butter), which is traditionally used in many Indian recipes. We recommend you buy a plant-based margarine with a high fat content (at least 70%).

Textured soya protein

Textured soya protein granules are a substitute for minced beef in our recipes for *shaaks* and stuffed potato fritters. You can use other textured plant-based proteins if you prefer, such as pea protein or sunflower protein, provided they are also in the form of small granules.

Draining plain firm tofu

As plain firm tofu contains a lot of water it needs to be drained so that it can absorb the flavours of the sauce or marinade in which it will be cooked. Although specialised tofu presses are available, you can achieve the same result by following these steps:

- Open the package while holding the tofu and press it over the sink to allow as much water as possible to drain off. Place a clean, absorbent tea towel on a large plate or chopping board.
- Cut the tofu into 1-cm slices and arrange on one half of the tea towel, then fold the other half back over the slices.
- Place a chopping board on top, then a heavy object on the board so that the weight presses down on all the slices evenly.
- Leave to drain for 20–30 minutes.

FRESH PRODUCE

Along with spices, garlic, ginger and onion, tomatoes and fresh herbs are basic ingredients in many Indian dishes.

- **Yellow onion** is usually added just after the *vaghar* has been made. It is fried over medium-low heat for around 10 minutes until the onions have softened nicely and become translucent. If you use them often, we recommend keeping a bag of onions (whole or chopped) in the freezer – it'll save you from popping to the shops if you run out!
- **Garlic and ginger**, in paste form (see p. 152 for recipes) or chopped very finely, are added just after the onions. As ginger is used more to flavour meat dishes, we use it less often than garlic, but it is still an important ingredient in our pulse-based recipes, as well as in certain condiments.
- As well as adding flavour, **tomatoes** release a cooking liquid that helps bind the spices (both whole and ground) and the garlic and ginger, before the other ingredients are added. When out of season, we replace fresh tomatoes with canned tomato concassée, reducing the quantity by a third. For example, if a recipe calls for 75 g of fresh tomatoes, we use 50 g of tomato concassée instead.
- **Fresh coriander** is the finishing touch to many dishes and also goes into various chutneys and fritters. Don't forget to freeze some so that it's on hand all year round (see p. 33 for tips).

DRY INGREDIENTS

Agar-agar
Agar-agar, a gelling powder extracted from red seaweed, can be used as a substitute for animal gelatine in many recipes. We use it in our rose and cardamom flan recipe.

Cashew nuts
Some of our recipes contain small quantities of cashew nuts, which add either creaminess (such as our pea *shaak* recipe) or a crunchy, gourmet touch (as in our *biryani*). However, we recommend buying cashew nuts that have been produced ethically and shelled mechanically. This is because the workers who shell cashew nuts by hand are exposed to caustic and allergenic substances that can cause burns, eye problems and sleep disorders.

Coconut milk
Although coconut milk is much less prevalent in northern Indian cuisine than in the south, it is still used in some of our traditional recipes, such as pea *shaak* and *akni*. To achieve creamy, fragrant results, we recommend using canned coconut milk that is full-fat and contains at least 85% coconut. Look for organic, fair-trade coconut milk with a 99% coconut content. As we very rarely use an entire can of coconut milk for our recipes, we recommend keeping the rest in the fridge for up to three days or in the freezer for a few months.

Jaggery
Jaggery, also known as *gur*, is an unrefined sugar made from either the mash extracted from sugar cane (the variety we use) or palm syrup. Available in block, chunk or coarse powder form, it can be used to impart sweet caramel and treacly notes to certain sweet or savoury dishes, such as our yoghurt and chickpea-flour soup.

Neutral cooking oil
Oil is an essential ingredient in Indian cooking. It releases the fat-soluble aromatic molecules that make up most spices, accentuating or toning down their flavours, bringing out the best qualities of each spice, allowing its fragrance to diffuse throughout the dish. Any neutral-tasting cooking oil can be used, such as deodorised sunflower or grapeseed oil.

Tomato paste
Used in most of our *shaak* recipes, tomato paste enhances the flavour of tomatoes. To bring out delicious caramelised notes, we recommend frying it well in hot oil.

Vermicelli, fried
Known as *plain bhujia* in Hindi, fried vermicelli are made from pulse flour (such as *chana* dal, mung beans, etc.) and various spices, with some varieties being thicker or spicier than others. They can be eaten as they are as a snack or added to dishes such as tomato *shaak* with fried vermicelli. They are also used as a topping on many typical Indian street food snacks.

Vermicelli, toasted wheat
Toasted wheat vermicelli look like capellini. But unlike Italian angel-hair pasta, Indian wheat vermicelli are toasted and therefore pre-cooked, giving them a slightly different texture, colour and taste. We use them in two of our sweet recipes: Toasted vermicelli with sultanas and Vermicelli with milk and vanilla.

Practical information

To help you achieve the best results from the recipes in this book, here is some practical information and advice on using the correct quantities of each ingredient, organising your cooking and understanding how to cook and store certain dishes and ingredients.

MEASUREMENTS

To measure spices, we use measuring spoons that correspond to the following amounts:

So-called teaspoons and tablespoons all have different capacities. We strongly recommend buying a set of four or five stainless steel measuring spoons (if you don't already own some) to measure out the small quantities required in our recipes.

- ⅛ teaspoon = 0.62 ml
- ¼ teaspoon = 1.25 ml
- ½ teaspoon = 2.5 ml
- 1 teaspoon = 5 ml
- 1 tablespoon = 15 ml
- 1 teaspoon garlic paste = 5 g
- 1 teaspoon ginger paste = 5 g

EQUIPMENT

Most of the equipment called for in this book is found in a well-equipped kitchen.

- **Measuring:** measuring cups and spoons, electronic scales.
- **Preparing:** chopping board, knives, potato peeler, grater, rolling pin.
- **Cooking:** saucepans, non-stick frying pan, sauté pan, stockpot, steamer basket.
- **Small appliances:** blender and food processor with an S-blade.
- An electric spice mill and/or mortar and pestle are only essential if you want to grind your own spices (see p. 22 for tips).

FRIED FOODS

To make the different types of fritters in this book, as well as *puris* and *biryani* potatoes, you'll need to have some kind of a fryer. If you're not familiar with frying, here are a few tips on how to fry safely.

Choose a saucepan with sufficiently high sides, making sure that the amount of oil called for in the recipe does not reach more than a third of the way up the sides.

Use a neutral-flavoured oil with a high smoke point that is suitable for frying, such as grapeseed or refined sunflower oil. Always follow the instructions on the label.

Foods to be fried should be immersed in hot, preheated oil and are usually cooked at a medium temperature or just a little higher. Remember to turn up the heat between frying, for example, batches of fritters, then allowing the oil to heat up for at least 1 minute before turning it down again and putting in the next batch.

To check if the oil is hot enough, dip a tiny piece of dough or bread in it; it should rise to the surface immediately, surrounded by tiny bubbles.

As a general rule, frying oil can be reused up to two or three times for the same type of food, provided it is filtered through a fine-mesh sieve to remove any impurities, then stored in an airtight container at room temperature, away from heat and light. If you notice a change in its appearance, taste or smell, dispose of it immediately.

STORING FOOD

Unless otherwise stated, all of the vegetable, pulse and rice dishes presented in this book can be stored in an airtight container in the fridge for up to three days.

If they have been made exclusively from fresh ingredients, i.e. without any frozen ingredients, they can be kept in the freezer for up to three months. Remember to label your containers with the contents and date of freezing. Leave at least 2 cm of space between the food and the lid to allow room for liquids to expand while freezing and to prevent the container from breaking.

SAVE TIME

Trying out new recipes can be time consuming, especially if you're unfamiliar with the type of dish, ingredients and/or techniques involved. Here are a few tips to help you simplify the process and incorporate our recipes into your everyday menus.

Start by prepping all the vegetables: wash, peel, seed and cut them according to the recipe instructions, then set them aside in separate bowls. To stop cut potatoes from turning brown, place them in a bowl of water until you're ready to use them.

Prepare your spices: most of our savoury recipes call for a combination of whole and ground spices, which are added at two different stages. Put the whole spices in one small bowl and the ground spices and salt in another. This will save you from having to measure out all your spices individually at the last minute, and allows you to move on to the next stage more quickly. Remember, only garam masala is usually added separately.

Prepare the spice base in advance: A *vaghar* (see p. 34 for explanations) is a mixture of oil and whole spices, to which onions, tomatoes, ground spices, salt, a garlic and ginger paste and/or chilli paste are usually added. It is the basis of most *shaak* and dal recipes. This base can be made one or two days in advance and stored in an airtight jar in the fridge. Simply reheat it and continue with the next step of the recipe. Even better, if you make double or triple the quantity and freeze it you'll have several bases ready in advance, and you'll save time when preparing specific dishes later on. Divide the *vaghar* into portions and freeze for up to three months. Remember to label your containers so you know which base corresponds to which dish, because they're all different!

Freeze fresh herbs, garlic, ginger, etc. Some of the fresh ingredients used in savoury recipes can be prepared in advance and in large quantities. This is particularly true of fresh herbs, such as coriander and mint. Wash, drain and dry them carefully by spreading them out on a clean tea towel for a few hours. Then, chop and store them in a jar in the freezer for up to three months. Use them as and when you need to by adding them directly to your dishes. Garlic, ginger and/or chilli pastes can be prepared in advance (see p. 152 for recipes) and chopped onions can also be frozen.

Prepare two or three *shaaks* or dals at a time. As most *shaak* and dal recipes call for similar basic ingredients, and the steps involved are much the same, it's easy to prepare two or three recipes at the same time. Once you've assembled the ingredients for one *vaghar*, you can easily cook a second or even a third in another pan. Of course, it takes longer than preparing a single dish, but it's still quicker than making the two dishes separately – that's the whole point of batch cooking!

A FEW DETAILS ABOUT LANGUAGE

Despite our best efforts to translate as many words as possible into English, some words simply have no equivalent in other languages. As a result, a few Gujarati words appear in our book. We hope the following explanations will help you to understand them:

- **Dal:** a word that applies to different types of pulses and also to the dish in which they are the star ingredient.
- ***Mithai*:** this refers to sweet dishes that are mainly served at the beginning of a meal rather than at the end. It can also be a food that is central in specific religious rituals and cultural celebrations. *Mithai* are not, by definition, simply 'desserts', and while there is nothing to stop us eating them as such, I personally prefer to translate *mithai* as 'sweets'.
- ***Shaak*:** the name for a cooked vegetable-based dish with a sauce, which can be made with or without meat.
- ***Vaghar*:** called *tarka* in Hindi, *vaghar* is a cooking technique that involves frying whole spices in oil to release their essential oils. This is usually the first step when preparing a *shaak* or a dal, but a *vaghar* can also be added as a finishing touch, to spice up a dal, a fritter batter or even a salad.

A FINAL TIP

When trying a recipe for the first time, read it right through to the end. Then, make sure you have all the ingredients and equipment, not to mention enough time, to ensure it turns out as it should. In our experience, being properly prepared is the key to stress-free, efficient and successful cooking!

Why are there no 'curries' in this book?

Although the word 'curry' refers to both a mixture of ground spices and a spiced-sauced dish typically found in Indian cuisine, the term did not actually originate in India. A golden yellow curry powder was created in the 18th century at the request of the British who had spent time in India and wanted to recreate – on their return 'home' – the flavours of the dishes they had enjoyed there. The word 'curry', which is used to describe most Indian dishes in the West, is also linked to colonialism as well as to this famous spice mix. Before the British started labelling all dishes containing curry powder as 'curries', Portuguese colonisers began describing Indian dishes as 'karis'. Today, the only use of the word 'curry' that makes any proper sense in English is with regard to curry leaves, a spice commonly used in Indian cuisine (see p. 17 for more information). In Hindi, these leaves are called *kari patta* and come from the Tamil word *kari*, which, in the past, was used to refer to a spicy sauce. However, the similarity between the Portuguese 'kari' and the British 'curry' is striking! This has resulted in the name of a single spice being used to denote both a mixture of spices and all the dishes of a country. Interestingly, although each region has its own specific language and every dish has a different name, not one of them actually contains curry powder!

Vegetables

નારિયેળ વાળા વટાણા – *Naryel vara vatana*

Pea *shaak* with coconut milk

Not sure which recipe from our book to try first? Look no further! Pea *shaak* with coconut milk is a very flavoursome and satisfying dish that everyone will love. It takes very little time to prepare and the ingredients are easy to store and have on hand. Without a doubt, this is the dish that I make most often – and all year round – from this book: That's the beauty of always having peas in the freezer.

Serves 4
Preparation time: 10 mins
Cooking time: 35 mins

90 g tomatoes (or 60 g tomato concassée)
30 g raw cashew nuts
3 tbsp neutral cooking oil
½ tsp black mustard seeds
6 curry leaves
1 tsp garlic paste
½ tsp ground cumin
½ tsp ground turmeric
½ tsp salt
450 g frozen peas (petits pois)
150 ml coconut milk (see p. 27 for tips)

Dice the fresh tomatoes. Grind the cashew nuts to a powder, then toast in a small frying pan until lightly browned.

Heat the oil in a saucepan over medium heat. Fry the whole spices (mustard seeds and curry leaves) for 1 minute, then add the garlic paste and fry for another minute.

Add the diced tomato, ground cashews, ground spices and salt. Cover and cook for 5 minutes or until the oil has risen to the surface.

Add the peas and 250 ml of boiling water. Cover and leave to cook for 15 minutes.

Stir in the coconut milk and continue cooking, half-covered, for 10 minutes, stirring regularly. Serve immediately.

Tips

- If you don't eat this dish immediately, the sauce will thicken. Remember to add a little water to dilute the sauce when you reheat it.
- You can also add diced potatoes (about 300 g), putting them in at the same time as the peas.
- Enjoy with plain rice, flatbread and the pickle of your choice.

બટેટા નુ શાક – *Bateta nou shaak*

Potato *shaak* with sesame seeds

This traditional Gujarati recipe features potatoes that are deliciously spiced up thanks to the acidity of the tamarind and the flavour of the toasted sesame seeds, as well as a blend of whole and ground spices. For an even better flavour, I recommend browning them well before adding the water.

Serves 6
Preparation time: 15 mins
Cooking time: 40 mins

- 1 kg waxy potatoes
- 110 g tomatoes (or 70 g tomato concassée)
- 6 tbsp neutral cooking oil
- 1 tsp black mustard seeds
- 2 tsp cumin seeds
- 10 small curry leaves
- 1 tbsp garlic paste
- ½ tsp salt
- 1 tsp ground coriander
- ½ tsp ground turmeric
- ½ tsp garam masala
- 1 tsp tamarind pulp
- 1 tsp white sesame seeds

Peel and cut the potatoes into 2-cm cubes. Dice the tomatoes.

Heat the oil in a frying pan or wok over medium heat. Fry the whole spices (seeds and curry leaves) for 1 minute, then add the garlic paste and fry for another minute.

Add the tomatoes, salt and ground spices (except the garam masala).

Cover and cook for 5 minutes or until the oil has risen to the surface.

Add the potatoes, garam masala and tamarind pulp. Cover and cook for a further 15 minutes, stirring regularly, until the potatoes are golden brown.

Pour in 150–250 ml of boiling water and cook, covered, for about 20 minutes or until the potatoes are cooked through.

Toast the sesame seeds in a dry frying pan, then add to the potatoes.

Mix well and serve.

Tips

- For a faster cooking time, cut the potatoes into half or quarter slices 5 mm thick.
- Serve with rice with lentils, chapatis (an Indian bread) and vegetable pickles.

ભાજી નુ શાક – *Bhaji nou shaak*

Spinach *shaak* with potatoes

Bhaji nou shaak **is one of the dishes that I most often ask my mother to make for me when I visit. As well as loving spinach and potatoes, I particularly like the unique flavours that the fenugreek seeds and leaves add to this dish.**

Serves 4
Preparation time: 15 mins
Cooking time: 55 mins

- 350 g fresh or frozen spinach
- 150 g waxy potatoes
- 150 g onions
- 75 g red pepper
- 3 tbsp neutral cooking oil
- ½ tsp fenugreek seeds
- 2 tsp garlic paste
- 1 tbsp tomato paste
- 150 g tomato concassée
- ½ tsp ground cumin
- ½ tsp ground turmeric
- ½ tsp sweet or hot chilli powder (optional, see p.16 for tips)
- ½ tsp salt
- 1 tbsp dried fenugreek leaves
- ½ tsp garam masala

Coarsely chop the fresh spinach. Peel and cut the potatoes into 2-cm cubes. Peel and finely chop the onion. Seed and cut the red pepper into 1-cm pieces.

In a large saucepan, heat the oil over medium-high heat and fry the fenugreek seeds for 1 minute, then the onions for 10 minutes.

Stir in the garlic paste and tomato paste and fry over medium heat for 1 minute.

Stir in the tomato concassée, ground spices (except the garam masala) and salt. Cover and cook for 5 minutes or until the oil has risen to the surface.

Next, add the potatoes, red pepper and the crushed fenugreek leaves and leave to cook, covered, for 5 minutes.

Add the spinach and 250 ml of boiling water and cook, covered, for 25 minutes, stirring regularly.

Add the garam masala, cook for a further 5 minutes, uncovered, and serve.

Tip

Serve with *khitchri*, your choice of flatbread and vegetable pickles.

સેવ ટમેટા નુ શાક – *Sev tameta nou shaak*

Tomato *shaak* with fried vermicelli

***Sev tameta nou shaak* is one of my mother's favourite childhood dishes. But it wasn't until I was writing this book that she introduced me to it – much to my delight. I love the contrasting textures in this dish as the tomatoes melt in your mouth, while the vermicelli are crunchy. Called *sev* in Gujarati, these vermicelli are made from split chickpea flour (*chana* dal) as well as a variety of spices. As it's ready in just 20 minutes, it's the perfect dish for those days when you're short of time.**

Serves 4
Preparation time: 20 mins
Cooking time: 15 mins

250 g tomatoes

1 fresh green chilli (optional, see p.16 for tips)

3 tbsp neutral cooking oil

½ tsp cumin seeds

½ tsp black mustard seeds

4 curry leaves

1 tsp garlic paste

½ tsp ginger paste

1 tsp tomato paste

¼ tsp ground turmeric

¼ tsp salt

½ tsp sugar

¼ tsp garam masala

100 g fried vermicelli (see p. 27 for tips)

For serving:

chickpea flour vermicelli

1 tbsp fresh coriander, chopped

Dice the tomatoes. Seed and chop the chilli.

In a large saucepan, heat the oil over medium heat and fry the whole spices (seeds and curry leaves) for 1 minute. Add the garlic and ginger pastes and the tomato paste and fry for another minute.

Add the tomatoes, green chilli, turmeric and salt. Cover and cook for 5 minutes or until the tomatoes have disintegrated.

Pour in 125 ml of boiling water, add the sugar and cook for a further 5 minutes. Add the garam masala and vermicelli and simmer for 2 minutes.

Take the pan off the heat and, just before serving, sprinkle the tomatoes with the vermicelli and chopped fresh coriander.

Tips

- Serve with *khitchri* and the flatbread of your choice.
- This dish can be prepared in advance. However, only add the vermicelli to the tomatoes right before serving.

કોબી નુ શાક – *Phali nou shaak*

Green bean *shaak* with peppers

The beans in this colourful dish are particularly tender and delicious as they absorb the flavour of the spices, and their texture contrasts nicely with the melt-in-the-mouth peppers. This is my favourite way of enjoying green beans in summer. But if you'd like to enjoy this dish all year round, simply use frozen green beans.

Serves 4
Preparation time: 15 mins
Cooking time: 45 mins

500 g fresh or frozen green beans
400 g red pepper
100 g tomatoes (or 65 g tomato concassée)
100 g onions
4 tbsp neutral cooking oil
1 tsp black mustard seeds
8 curry leaves
1 tsp garlic paste
1 tsp ginger paste
1 tbsp tomato paste
chilli, chopped, paste or powder (optional, see p.16 for tips)
2 tsp ground coriander
1 tsp ground cumin
¼ tsp ground turmeric
½ tsp salt
1 tsp garam masala

For serving:
4 tbsp fresh coriander, chopped

Top and tail the green beans. Seed and cut the red pepper into strips. Dice the tomatoes. Peel and finely chop the onion.

In a frying pan, heat the oil over medium heat and fry the whole spices (mustard seeds and curry leaves) for 1 minute, then add the onion and fry over medium-low heat for about 10 minutes. Fry the garlic and ginger pastes, tomato paste and chilli for 1 minute.

Add the diced tomato, ground spices (except the garam masala) and salt. Cover and cook for 5 minutes or until the oil has risen to the surface.

Add the green beans and red pepper strips and cook, covered, for 25 minutes, stirring halfway through cooking.

Add the garam masala and cook for a further 5 minutes.

Sprinkle with the chopped fresh coriander just before serving.

Tips

- For a more colourful dish, use a mix of red, yellow and orange peppers.
- Serve with rice with lentils or your choice of flatbread.

તોફુ વારી ક્રીમી ભાજી – *Tofu vari creamy bhaji*

Creamed spinach and tofu

My creamed spinach and tofu is inspired by *palak paneer*, a creamy dish made with blended spinach and cubes of cheese (*paneer*), traditionally made from raw buffalo milk. It's not a dish my family makes, and I actually first tried it in England. In fact, it was during the eight years I that lived there that I discovered other Indian cuisines. In my version of this dish, I have replaced the *paneer* with tofu, the cream made from animal milk with cashew nuts, and the fresh tomatoes with tomato sauce to create a dish with a thicker texture and an even tastier flavour.

Serves 4
Soaking time: 4 hrs
Preparation time: 15 mins
Cooking time: 50 mins

For the tofu:

300 g firm plain tofu
1 tbsp neutral cooking oil
½ tsp salt
1 tsp garam masala

For the creamed spinach:

100 g raw cashew nuts
400 g fresh or frozen spinach
100 g onions
10 g garlic
5 g ginger
3 tbsp neutral cooking oil
1 tsp mustard seeds
½ tsp cumin seeds
1 tbsp tomato paste
100 g tomato sauce
½ tsp sweet or hot chilli powder (optional, see p.16 for tips)
½ tsp salt
2 tsp garam masala

Soak the cashew nuts in a bowl of water for 4 hours, then drain well. Drain the tofu for 20 minutes (see p. 26 for tips).

Coarsely chop the fresh spinach. Peel and finely chop the garlic and ginger.

In a large saucepan, heat the oil over medium-high heat and fry the whole spices (mustard and cumin seeds) for 1 minute. Add the cashew nuts and fry for a further 2 minutes. Add the tomato paste, garlic and ginger and fry for 1 minute.

Stir in the tomato sauce, chilli and salt and cook, covered, for 3 minutes or until the oil has risen to the surface.

Turn down the heat to medium and pour in 500 ml of boiling water, then put in as much spinach as possible. Stir, cover and wait until the spinach has wilted before adding the rest.

Once all the spinach has been added, continue cooking, covered, for 25 minutes. Add the garam masala at the end.

Meanwhile, cut the tofu into 1.5-cm cubes, or tear into equivalent-sized pieces.

Heat the oil in a frying pan over medium-high heat, add the tofu pieces and brown evenly all over for 3–4 minutes. Add the salt and garam masala, mix well, turn off the heat and set aside.

Put the spinach mixture in a blender and whiz until smooth. Pour the creamed spinach back into the saucepan, stir in the browned tofu pieces and cook, covered, over low heat, for about 10 minutes.

Tips

- In this recipe, I like there to be more sauce than tofu, but feel free to add 100–200 g of extra tofu if you wish.
- This recipe is best prepared the day before to allow the tofu to absorb the flavours of the sauce. To achieve a texture similar to *paneer*, boil the tofu pieces for around 10 minutes before browning them. This will give them the slightly rubbery texture of this Indian cheese.
- Serve with plain basmati rice or naan.

રીંગણા ભરથુ – *Ringna barthou*

Grilled aubergine mash

Ringna barthou **is a dish I make mainly at the end of summer or in early autumn, when it gets cool enough to switch the oven on without turning the kitchen into a sauna. Roasted whole in the oven, the aubergines become silky and, after being mashed and fried with onions, tomatoes and various spices, the result is a very tasty dish that can be eaten hot or cold. For a little extra creaminess and a touch of acidity, add some yoghurt.**

Serves 4
Preparation time: 15 mins
Cooking time: 1 hr 10 mins

750 g aubergines + a little extra oil for brushing
150 g tomatoes (or 100 g tomato concassée)
200 g red, green and/or yellow peppers
175 g yellow onions
3 tbsp neutral cooking oil
3 cm cassia bark (approximately)
1 tsp garlic paste
1 tsp tomato paste
chilli, chopped, paste or powder (optional, see p.16 for tips)
½ tsp ground turmeric
¼ tsp ground coriander
¼ tsp ground cumin
¼ tsp garam masala
½ tsp salt
1 spring onion (optional)
50 g plain soya yoghurt (optional)

For serving:
4 tbsp fresh coriander, chopped

Preheat the oven to 200°C/180°C fan/gas mark 6.

Wash and dry the aubergines, slit the skin lengthways, brush with oil and place in the oven for around 40 minutes or until the flesh is soft.

Dice the tomatoes. Seed and dice the pepper/s. Peel and finely chop the onions and spring onion.

In a saucepan, heat the oil over medium heat and fry the cassia for 1 minute, then fry the onions over medium-low heat for about 10 minutes. Add the garlic paste, tomato paste and chilli and fry for 1 minute over medium heat.

Add the diced tomato, ground spices and salt and cook, covered, for 5 minutes or until the oil has risen to the surface.

Peel the aubergines, remove the stalks and coarsely mash the flesh with a fork or potato masher. Stir the mashed aubergine flesh into the ingredients in the saucepan, then cover and simmer for 5 minutes.

Lastly, add the spring onion and yoghurt, mix well and continue cooking for a few minutes.

Sprinkle with the chopped fresh coriander just before serving.

Tip

If you eat this dish hot, serve with rice with lentils, chapatis, parathas or puris. You can also enjoy it cold, on toast or in a sandwich. And lastly, although it's more unusual, I really like using *barthou* as a tart filling or for stuffing turnovers.

રીંગણા નુ શાક આખી ચણા દાળ સાથે – *Ringna nou shaak akhi chana dal saté*

Aubergines with split chickpeas

This is a particularly hearty and comforting dish that I like to prepare in early autumn. Peppers and aubergines are still in season, and we're starting to get our jumpers and coats out. Given the time it takes to cook this dish, I always make large quantities of it to freeze, and that way it can be enjoyed in winter too.

Serves 6–8
Soaking time: 12 hrs
Preparation time: 15 mins
Cooking time: 1 hr 25 mins

200 g *chana* dal (split chickpeas, dry weight)
150 g aubergines
100 g tomatoes (or 65 g tomato concassée)
200 g red peppers
200 g onions
60 ml neutral cooking oil
1 tsp black mustard seeds
12 curry leaves
1 tsp garlic paste
2 tsp tomato paste
chilli, chopped, paste or powder (optional, see p.16 for tips)
1 tsp dried fenugreek leaves
½ tsp ground cumin
1 tbsp ground coriander
½ tsp ground turmeric
1 tsp salt
1 tsp garam masala

For serving:
4 tbsp fresh coriander, chopped

Rinse the split chickpeas and leave to soak in plenty of cold water for 12 hours. Rinse them again.

Cut the aubergines and tomatoes into 2-cm cubes. Seed and cut the pepper into equal-sized pieces. Peel and finely chop the onion.

In a large frying pan, heat the oil over medium heat and the whole spices (mustard seeds and curry leaves) for 1 minute, then add the onion and fry over medium-low heat for about 10 minutes. Add the garlic, tomato paste and chilli, and fry for 1 minute.

Add the dried and crushed fenugreek leaves, ground spices (except the garam masala), salt, tomatoes and pepper. Cover and cook for 5 minutes or until the oil has risen to the surface.

Stir in the split chickpeas, cover and cook over medium-low heat for 5 minutes. Add the garam masala and 550 ml of boiling water and continue cooking, covered, for 30 minutes.

Lastly, add the aubergines and cook, covered, for a further 30 minutes.

Sprinkle with the chopped fresh coriander just before serving.

Tip

Serve with plain or spiced basmati rice, or your choice of flatbread.

કોબી ના ફુલ નુ શાકુ – *Kobi na foul nou shaak*

Cauliflower *shaak*

In this recipe, the flavour of the cauliflower is mellowed by a sauce that includes cinnamon, mustard seeds and curry leaves, which this vegetable absorbs as it cooks. Adding water at the end of the cooking process stops the cauliflower from becoming soggy. Even those who don't usually like cauliflower fall for it in this recipe.

Serves 3
Preparation time: 10 mins
Cooking time: 40 mins

- 150 g tomatoes (or 100 g tomato concassée)
- 25 g red pepper
- 5 tbsp neutral cooking oil
- 3 cm cassia bark
- 1 tsp black mustard seeds
- 6 curry leaves
- chilli, chopped, paste or powder (optional, see p.16 for tips)
- ½ tsp ground cumin
- ½ tsp ground coriander
- ½ tsp ground turmeric
- ½ tsp salt
- 200 g fresh or frozen cauliflower florets

Dice the tomatoes. Seed and cut the pepper into dice.

Heat the oil in a saucepan over medium-high heat and fry the whole spices (cassia, mustard seeds and curry leaves) for 1 minute. Add the tomatoes, chilli, ground spices and salt and cook, covered, for 5 minutes or until the oil has risen to the surface.

Stir in the cauliflower and pepper, cover and continue cooking for 10 minutes.

Pour in 250 ml of boiling water, stir and cook over medium heat for 20 minutes before serving.

Tip

Serve with *khitchri*, chapatis or parathas and chutney.

ભીંડા નુ શાક – *Bhinda nou shaak*

Okra *shaak*

Okra is a pod that is roughly the same length as a green bean, but thicker. It has downy skin and contains small mucilaginous seeds. India – and the Gujarat region in particular – has become the largest producer of this West African vegetable. In the UK, you can buy okra in grocery shops specialising in Asian or African products, and even in some supermarkets.

Serves 4
Preparation time: 15 mins
Cooking time: 1 hr

- 100 g potatoes
- 135 g tomatoes (or 90 g tomato concassée)
- 75 g red pepper
- 500 g okra
- 70 g onions
- 4 tbsp neutral cooking oil
- 1 cm, approx., cassia bark
- ½ tsp black mustard seeds
- 1 tsp garlic paste
- 1 tbsp tomato paste
- chilli, chopped, paste or powder (optional, see p.16 for tips)
- 2 tsp ground coriander
- 1 tsp ground cumin
- ¼ tsp ground turmeric
- ½ tsp salt
- ½ tsp garam masala

Peel and cut the potatoes into half moons about 5 mm thick. Dice the tomatoes. Seed and slice the pepper. Top and tail the okra. Peel and finely chop the onion.

In a saucepan, heat the oil over medium-high heat and fry the whole spices (cassia and mustard seeds) for 1 minute, then add the onion and fry over medium-low heat for about 10 minutes. Add the garlic, tomato paste and chilli and fry for 1 minute over medium heat.

Add the tomatoes, ground spices (except the garam masala) and salt and cook, covered, for 5 minutes or until the oil has risen to the surface.

Stir in the peppers and potatoes and cook for about 5 minutes or until the potatoes start to brown. Add the okra and continue cooking, covered, for 15 minutes or until the oil has risen to the surface.

Pour in 125 ml of boiling water and cook, covered, for about 20 minutes (cooking times may vary according to the type of okra and potato).

When the vegetables are cooked through, add the garam masala, mix well and serve.

Tips

- Serve with rice with lentils, chapatis or parathas and vegetable pickles.
- To avoid squashing the okra, stir the mixture gently as it cooks.

કોબી નુ શાક – *Kobi nou shaak*

White cabbage *shaak*

This is one of the few recipes in which I actually enjoy eating cabbage! The spices mellow its distinctive flavour while enhancing its best qualities. Served alongside rice with lentils, puris and vegetable pickles, it's a real treat.

Serves 4
Preparation time: 10 mins
Cooking time: 55 mins

- 250 g white cabbage
- 75 g tomatoes (or 50 g tomato concassée)
- 125 g onions
- 2 tbsp neutral cooking oil
- 3 cm cassia bark
- ¼ tsp fenugreek seeds
- ½ tsp black mustard seeds
- 5 curry leaves
- 1 tsp garlic paste (or 5 g crushed garlic)
- 1½ tsp tomato paste
- chilli, chopped, paste or powder (optional, see p.16 for tips)
- 2 tsp ground coriander
- ½ tsp ground cumin
- ½ tsp salt

Cut the cabbage into strips and the tomatoes into dice. Peel and finely chop the onion.

In a large saucepan, heat the oil over medium-high heat and fry the whole spices (cassia, seeds and curry leaves) for 1 minute, then add the onion and fry over medium-low heat for 10 minutes. Add the garlic paste, tomato paste and chilli and fry for 1 minute.

Add the ground spices, salt and diced tomato. Cover and cook over medium heat for about 5 minutes or until the oil has risen to the surface.

Stir in the white cabbage and cook, covered, for 5 minutes.

Pour in 250 ml of boiling water and cook over medium heat, covered, for 30 minutes, stirring regularly. Enjoy!

Tip

You can use red cabbage instead of white cabbage, or even a mixture of both.

Pulses

મસૂર દાળ – *Masoor dal*

Brown lentil dal

The word dal is used in India to refer to pulses as well as dishes whose main ingredient is lentils or beans. Depending on the recipe, a dal can be quite thick or a little more runny, chunky or creamy, and may contain vegetables. A fairly filling dish, dals are high in protein. Throughout the week, we prepare a variety of dals that are usually served with plain, spiced or coconut milk rice and a vegetable *shaak* to ensure that each meal is balanced.

Serves 4–6
Soaking time: 12 hrs
Preparation time: 10 mins
Cooking time: 1 hr 10 mins

- 200 g whole *masoor* lentils (unhulled)
- 75 g carrots
- 125 g tomatoes (or 80 g tomato concassée)
- 140 g onions
- 3 tbsp neutral cooking oil
- 2 cloves
- 10 curry leaves
- 2 tsp garlic paste
- 1 tsp ginger paste
- 1 tbsp tomato paste
- chilli, chopped, paste or powder (optional, see p.16 for tips)
- 1 tsp salt
- 1 pinch ground asafoetida (optional)
- 1 tsp ground cumin
- 1 tsp ground coriander
- 1 tsp garam masala
- 1 tsp lemon juice
- 1 tsp plant-based margarine

For serving:

6 tbsp fresh coriander, chopped

Rinse the lentils, leave to soak in plenty of water for 12 hours, drain and then rinse again.

Peel and slice the carrots into thin rounds. Dice the tomatoes. Peel and finely chop the onions.

Place the lentils and 750 ml of water in a saucepan, bring to the boil over medium-high heat, then cover and leave to cook over medium-low heat for about 20 minutes or until the lentils are tender.

In a large frying pan or saucepan, heat the oil over medium heat and fry the whole spices (cloves and curry leaves) for 1 minute. Add the onion and fry over medium-low heat for 10 minutes. Add the garlic and ginger pastes, tomato paste and fry for another minute.

Add the salt, tomatoes and all the ground spices (except the garam masala). Cover and cook for 5 minutes or until the oil has risen to the surface.

Add the lentils – together with the cooking water – and the carrots, and cook, covered, over medium–low heat for 30 minutes.

Add the garam masala, lemon juice and margarine, stir well and continue cooking, uncovered, for 2 minutes.

Serve the dal sprinkled with the chopped fresh coriander.

Tips

- Serve with your choice of flatbread, coconut or spiced rice and vegetable pickles.
- If you can't find unhulled *masoor* lentils, you can use other types of brown or green lentils, such as Puy lentils.

કબાળુ ની દાળ – *Kabarou ni dal*

Giant white bean dal

The beans used in this recipe are known as butter beans, a tasty variety of pulse that melts in the mouth and is one of my favourites. This dal can be enjoyed in different ways: leave the beans whole for extra texture, or blend them at the end of cooking for a creamy version.

Serves 4–6
Soaking time: 24 hrs
Preparation time: 10 mins
Cooking time: 1 hr 40 mins

- 250 g large white beans (butter beans)
- 75 g tomatoes (or 50 g tomato concassée)
- 90 g onions
- 4 tbsp neutral cooking oil
- ½ tsp fenugreek seeds
- 1 tsp garlic paste
- 1 tbsp tomato paste
- chilli, chopped, paste or powder (optional, see p.16 for tips)
- 1 pinch ground asafoetida (optional)
- 1 tsp ground coriander
- ¼ tsp ground cumin
- ½ tsp salt
- ½ tsp garam masala

For serving:
4 tbsp fresh coriander, chopped

Rinse the beans, leave to soak in plenty of water for 12 hours, drain, rinse and leave to soak in plenty of water for a further 12 hours.

Place the rinsed and drained beans and 1 litre of water in a saucepan. Bring to the boil over medium-high heat, then cook over medium-low heat, covered, for about 45 minutes or until the beans are tender.

Dice the tomatoes. Peel and finely chop the onions.

In a large saucepan, heat the oil over medium heat and fry the fenugreek seeds for 1 minute, then add the onion and fry over medium-low heat for 10 minutes. Add the garlic paste, tomato paste and chilli and fry for 1 minute.

Add the ground spices (except the garam masala), salt and tomatoes. Leave to cook, covered, for 5 minutes or until the oil has risen to the surface.

Add the cooked white beans with their cooking water and 250 ml of boiling water. Cover and leave to cook over medium-low heat for 30 minutes.

Add the garam masala and cook, uncovered, for a further 5 minutes.

Serve sprinkled with the chopped fresh coriander.

Tips

- Serve with your choice of flatbread, coconut or spiced rice and vegetable pickles.
- For an even more delicious dal, add 100 ml of coconut milk (see p. 27 for tips) 10 minutes before the end of the cooking time, adding 150 ml instead of 250 ml of boiling water.

ચણાની દાળ – *Chana dal*

Split chickpea dal

Of all the recipes in this book, this is definitely the creamiest. Split and hulled *chana* dal become incredibly silky, as long as they are soaked and cooked long enough. The result is wonderfully comforting, especially when it's cold outside!

Serves 4
Soaking time: 24 hrs
Preparation time: 10 mins
Cooking time: 1 hr 40 mins

- 200 g *chana* dal (split, hulled chickpeas)
- 80 g tomatoes (or 50 g tomato concassée)
- 65 g onions
- 3 tbsp neutral cooking oil
- ½ tsp fenugreek seeds
- 10 curry leaves
- 1 tsp garlic paste
- chilli, chopped, paste or powder (optional, see p.16 for tips)
- 1 tsp salt
- 1 pinch ground asafoetida (optional)
- 1 tsp ground coriander
- ½ tsp ground cumin
- ½ tsp ground turmeric
- ½ tsp garam masala

For serving:

- 4 tbsp fresh coriander, chopped

Rinse the *chana* dal and leave to soak in plenty of water for 12 hours. Drain and rinse, then leave to soak for a further 12 hours in plenty of water.

Place the rinsed and drained chickpeas and 750 ml of water in a saucepan. Bring to the boil over medium-high heat, then cook, covered, over medium-low heat for about 45 minutes or until the chickpeas are tender.

Dice the tomatoes. Peel and finely chop the onions.

In a large sauté pan or saucepan, heat the oil over medium heat and fry the whole spices (fenugreek seeds and curry leaves) for 1 minute, then add the onion and fry over medium-low heat for 10 minutes. Add the garlic and chilli pastes and fry for 1 minute. Then add the salt, tomatoes and ground spices (except the garam masala), and leave to cook, covered for 5 minutes or until the oil has risen to the surface.

Add the *chana* dal together with the cooking water, and cook, covered, over medium-low heat for 30 minutes.

Add the garam masala and cook, uncovered, for a further 5 minutes.

Serve the dal sprinkled with the chopped fresh coriander.

Tip

Serve with your choice of flatbread, coconut or spiced rice and vegetable pickles.

મિક્સ દાળ – *Mix dal*

Four-pulse dal

For our final dal recipe, we recommend combining four types of hulled pulses: *masoor*, mung beans, chickpeas, and split pigeon peas as each pulse brings a special flavour, colour and texture to the dish.

Serves 4–6
Soaking time: 12 hrs
Preparation time: 10 mins
Cooking time: 1 hr 40 mins

60 g hulled *masoor* lentils (or red lentils)
60 g split, hulled mung beans
30 g *chana* dal (split, hulled chickpeas)
30 g *toor* dal (split, hulled pigeon peas)
100 g tomatoes (or 65 g tomato concassée)
70 g onions
4 tbsp neutral cooking oil
2 cm cassia bark
½ tsp black mustard seeds
½ tsp fenugreek seeds
5 curry leaves
1 tsp garlic paste
½ tsp tomato paste
chilli, chopped, paste or powder (optional, see p.16 for tips)
1 tsp salt
1 pinch ground asafoetida (optional)
1.5 tsp ground coriander
½ tsp ground cumin
½ tsp ground turmeric
½ tsp garam masala

For serving:
4 tbsp fresh coriander, chopped

Rinse the pulses, leave to soak in plenty of water for 12 hours, drain and rinse again.

Place the pulses and 625 ml of water in a saucepan. Bring to the boil over medium-high heat and cook for around 45 minutes or until the pulses are tender.

Dice the tomatoes. Peel and finely chop the onion.

In a large saucepan, heat the oil over medium heat and fry the whole spices (cassia, seeds and curry leaves) for 1 minute, then add the onion and fry over medium-low heat for 10 minutes. Add the garlic paste, tomato paste and chilli and fry over medium heat for 1 minute.

Add the salt, tomatoes and ground spices (except the garam masala) and cook, covered, for 5 minutes or until the oil has risen to the surface.

Add the pulses together with their cooking water and cook, covered, over medium-low heat for 30 minutes.

Add the garam masala and cook, uncovered, for a further 5 minutes.

Serve the dal sprinkled with the chopped fresh coriander.

Tip

Serve with your choice of flatbread, coconut or spiced rice and vegetable pickles.

ફુટેલા મગ નુ શાક – *Foutela mug nou shaak*

Sprouted mung bean *shaak*

Also known as green soya beans, mung beans are available in three forms: whole (mung beans), split (mung dal *chilka*) or split and hulled (mung dal). For this recipe, we use them whole and sprouted. Generally speaking, to maximise the nutritional value of sprouted seeds, it's best to avoid cooking them. That's why I prefer to simply infuse the sprouted beans in the spicy base when it's ready, rather than cooking them for as long as we would for other *shaaks*. However, if you like, you can cook them over very low heat.

Serves 4
Soaking time: 48 hrs
Germination: 48 hrs
Preparation time: 10 mins
Cooking time: 15 mins
Resting time: 10 mins

100 g mung beans (350 g sprouted)
150 g tomatoes (or 100 g tomato concassée)
75 g red pepper
3 tbsp neutral cooking oil
1 cm cassia bark
1 tsp cumin seeds
½ tsp black mustard seeds
10 curry leaves
1 tsp garlic paste
chilli, chopped, paste or powder (optional, see p.16 for tips)
1 tsp ground coriander
½ tsp ground cumin
¼ tsp ground turmeric
½ tsp salt

For serving:
4 tbsp fresh coriander, chopped

Soak the beans in plenty of water for 48 hours. After 12 hours, drain and rinse them, and leave to soak again in fresh water for a further 12 hours.

Drain and rinse the beans, then leave to drain in a large sprouting jar on its stand for 24 hours, rinsing the seeds well after 12 hours. At the end of the germination period, rinse the sprouted beans one last time and place them in a cool, dry, closed container for up to 48 hours.

Dice the tomatoes. Seed and cut the pepper into 1-cm cubes.

In a large saucepan, heat the oil over medium heat and fry the whole spices (cassia, seeds and curry leaves) for 1 minute, then add the garlic paste and fry for another minute.

Add the tomatoes, chilli, ground spices and salt. Cook over medium heat, covered, for 5 minutes or until the oil has risen to the surface.

Add the pepper and 250 ml of boiling water, cover again and cook for 5 minutes.

Remove from the heat, stir in the sprouted beans and leave to infuse for about 10 minutes.

Sprinkle with the chopped fresh coriander and serve immediately.

Tips

- Serve with your choice of flatbread, spiced or coconut rice, green chutney or vegetable pickles (see pp. 146 and 149).
- In order for the seeds to germinate properly, the jars used must be quite big, and you shouldn't fill them more than a third of the way up. You can definitely use more than one jar at a time for the germination phase. If you don't have a germination jar, use a large glass jar. Place a clean, fine tea towel on top (don't use the jar's own lid) and hold it place with a rubber band. The jar then needs to be kept tilted with the top facing downwards to allow the excess water to drain into a container, but be careful not to let the beans pile up.

જીરા વારુ તોફુ – *Jeera varou tofu*

Cumin tofu

I used to love my mother's cumin chicken, but this version, made with tofu, is just as delicious. In this easy-to-make dish, cumin is used in three different ways – whole, ground and coarsely crushed in a mortar and pestle – and it goes wonderfully with tofu.

Serves 4
Resting time: 30 mins
Preparation time: 5 mins
Cooking time: 25 mins

400 g plain firm tofu
120 g tomatoes (or 80 g tomato concassée)
3 tbsp neutral cooking oil
3½ tsp cumin seeds
3 cm cassia bark
1 tsp garlic paste
1 tsp ginger paste
½ tsp ground turmeric
½ tsp toasted, ground cumin
¾ tsp salt

For serving:
2 tbsp fresh coriander, chopped

Drain the tofu (see p. 26 for explanations) for 30 minutes.

Tear the tofu into 1.5-cm pieces. Dice the tomatoes.

In a wok, heat the oil over medium-high heat and fry 2½ teaspoons of the cumin seeds with the cassia until fragrant (about 2 minutes). Add the garlic and ginger pastes and fry for another minute.

Add the tomatoes, turmeric, ground cumin and salt, and cook, covered, for about 5 minutes or until the oil has risen to the surface.

Add the pieces of tofu and toss to coat each piece all over. Cover and continue cooking for 10 minutes, stirring regularly, so that the tofu cubes are nicely browned.

Deglaze with 80 ml of boiling water and stir. Crush the remaining teaspoon of cumin seeds in a mortar and pestle. Add to the wok, stir and cook, covered, for 5 minutes.

Serve sprinkled with the chopped fresh coriander.

Tip

Try it served with coconut milk rice, vegetable pickles (see p. 165) and a date and tamarind chutney (see p. 151).

કોથમીર વારુ તોફુ – *Kothmir varou tofu*

Coriander tofu

In this recipe, I've replaced the chicken with tofu, combining it with a creamy cashew and coriander sauce that I particularly like. To ensure the tofu fully absorbs the flavours of the sauce, I strongly recommend using a firm, natural tofu that has been frozen and then defrosted. As tofu freezes, the water inside it turns into tiny crystals. As it thaws, the tofu becomes spongy, allowing the minute holes to quickly and efficiently soak up all kinds of marinades.

Serves 4
Freezing time: 24 hrs
Defrosting time: 24–36 hrs
Preparation time: 15 mins
Resting time: 30 mins
Cooking time: 25 mins

400 g plain firm tofu
100 g green pepper
50 g tomatoes (or 30 g tomato concassée)
1 small clove of garlic (2.5 g)
100 g raw cashew nuts
2 tbsp plant-based margarine
85 g fresh coriander
1 green chilli (optional)
1 tsp salt
1 tbsp neutral cooking oil
50 ml soya cream

Begin preparing the tofu at least 48 hours before you want to make this dish. Put the tofu in the freezer for 24 hours, then in the fridge for 24–36 hours to defrost.

Once the tofu has defrosted, drain it for 30 minutes (see p. 26 for tips), then tear it into pieces about 1.5 cm square.

Meanwhile, seed and cut the pepper into 3 pieces. Cut the tomato into quarters. Peel and finely chop the garlic. Grind the cashew nuts to a powder, then fry in the melted margarine over medium heat until golden brown, about 3 minutes. Wash, dry and coarsely chop the fresh coriander, including the stems if tender.

Put the coriander, pepper, green chilli, tomato, garlic, 100 ml of water and the salt in a blender and whiz until smooth and creamy.

Heat the oil in a wok over medium-high heat and fry the tofu for a few minutes until lightly browned.

Add the coriander sauce, soya cream and ground cashew nuts. Stir and leave to cook, covered, over low heat for around 20 minutes. Enjoy!

Tips

- Serve with any flatbread, plain rice or coconut milk rice, date and tamarind chutney (see p.151) or carrot pickles.
- If you haven't had time to prepare the tofu in advance, you can use unfrozen firm tofu instead. If that is the case, I recommend marinating the tofu in the sauce (without the cream or cashew nuts) for anywhere between 2 and 24 hours before heating the dish and adding the cream and ground cashew nuts.

તંદૂરી તોફુ – *Tandoori tofu*

Tandoori tofu

This recipe, inspired by tandoori chicken, is traditionally cooked in a tandoor, a typical Indian clay oven. Whether roasted whole or in pieces, or grilled on skewers, what makes tandoori chicken taste so special is the yoghurt-based mixture it is marinated in. In this recipe, I have replaced the chicken with defrosted tofu cubes (see p. 75 for explanations) and the animal milk yoghurt with Greek-style soya yoghurt. The result is deliciously soft yet roasted cubes infused with tandoori spices. Serve with naan (see p. 129), raita (see p. 142), *kachumber* (see p. 145), green chutney (see pp. 146 and 149) and/or vegetable pickles (see p. 165).

Serves 4–6
Freezing time: 48 hrs
Defrosting time: 24–36 hrs
Preparation time: 5 mins
Marinating time: 1 hr
Cooking time: 30 mins

400 g firm plain tofu
60 g tandoori paste (see p. 157 for recipe)
120 g Greek-style soya yoghurt
¼ tsp salt
neutral cooking oil

Leave the tofu in the freezer for at least 48 hours, then transfer to the fridge for a further 24–36 hours to defrost.

Once the tofu has defrosted, leave to drain for 30 minutes (see p. 26 for tips), then cut into pieces about 2 cm square and 5 mm thick.

Mix the tandoori paste with the yoghurt and salt, coat the tofu pieces with it and leave to rest in the fridge for 1 hour.

Preheat the oven to 200°C/180°C fan/gas mark 6/7. Arrange the cubes on a baking tray and roast for 15 minutes. Turn the tofu pieces over and continue roasting for a further 15 minutes. Allow to cool and enjoy!

Tips

- If you haven't had time to prepare the tofu in advance, you can use firm tofu that has not been frozen and start with the step on draining the tofu. I recommend marinating the tofu for 2–4 hours.
- Feel free to add pieces of onion and bell pepper to the marinade along with the tofu, but if you do, be sure to make extra marinade.
- For an even crispier result, place the tofu under the grill for 1–2 minutes at the end of roasting, or grill it on a barbecue. Heat up any leftovers in a little oil in a frying pan to make the tofu even crispier.

મક્સ તોફુ – *Mix tofu*

Scrambled tofu

Before I went vegan, I liked eggs cooked in every way, especially my mother's *beda nou shaak*, a kind of scrambled egg flavoured with all sorts of spices, but also shallots and spring onions. This plant-based alternative uses a combination of firm and silken tofu to recreate the texture of scrambled eggs. The addition of *kala namak* salt imparts a slightly sulphurous, eggy aroma and flavour to the dish.

Serves 6
Resting time: 30 mins
Preparation time: 15 mins
Marinating time: 30 mins
Cooking time: 25 mins

- 400 g plain firm tofu
- 400 g silken tofu
- 100 g tomatoes (or 65 g tomato concassée)
- 1 green chilli (optional, see p.16 for tips)
- 75 g shallots
- 75 g spring onions
- 5 tbsp neutral cooking oil
- 5 mm cassia bark
- ½ tsp cumin seeds
- ½ tsp ground coriander
- ¾ tsp ground cumin
- ½ tsp garam masala
- ¼ tsp chilli powder (optional)
- 1 pinch ground cinnamon
- ½ tsp *kala namak* or fine salt

For the marinade:

- ¼ tsp ground turmeric
- ¼ tsp paprika
- ¼ tsp chilli powder (optional)
- ½ tsp salt

For serving:

- 3 tbsp fresh coriander, chopped

Drain the plain firm tofu (see p. 26 for tips) for 30 minutes and the silken tofu for 10 minutes, placing it gently in a fine-mesh sieve over a bowl.

Over a medium-sized bowl, use your fingers to crumble the firm tofu. Add the silken tofu and the marinade spices. Mix well and leave to rest in the fridge for at least 30 minutes.

Dice the tomatoes. Seed and finely chop the chilli. Peel and finely chop the shallots and spring onions.

In a large frying pan, heat the oil over medium heat and fry the whole spices (cassia and cumin seeds) for 1 minute, then add the shallots, spring onions and chilli and fry for 5 minutes. Add the tomatoes, ground spices and salt and cook, covered, for 5 minutes or until the oil has risen to the surface.

Add the tofu mixture. Stir everything together, then leave to cook over medium-high heat, uncovered, for 5 minutes, without stirring. As soon as the tofu starts to brown underneath, stir regularly for about 7 minutes or until the result is well scrambled and is neither watery nor overcooked.

Sprinkle with the chopped fresh coriander just before serving.

Tips

- Enjoy with your choice of vegetable pickles and a date and tamarind chutney (see p. 151).
- Scrambled tofu also works really well as a sandwich filling.
- The spiced tofu mixture can be made the day before and left to rest in the fridge for up to 24 hours.

સોયા ચંક્સ નુ શાક – *Soya chunks nou shaak*

Textured soya protein *shaak*

This recipe is a substitute for the *khima nou shaak* I often enjoyed as a child. Traditionally made with minced beef, this is a dish I used to love to eat with chapatis, in an omelette or in a grilled cheese sandwich – the latter was one of my favourite meals to take on school outings. I'm happy to be able to rediscover the flavours of this dish by replacing the ground beef with textured soya protein granules.

Serves 4–6
Preparation time: 15 mins
Cooking time: 45 mins

100 g tomatoes (or 65 g tomato concassée)
40 g red pepper
160 g onions
4 tbsp neutral cooking oil
3 cm cassia bark
½ tsp cumin seeds
1 tsp garlic paste
1 tsp ginger paste
1 tbsp tomato paste
chilli, chopped, paste or powder (optional, see p.16 for tips)
150 g tomato concassée
2 tsp ground coriander
½ tsp ground cumin
¼ tsp ground turmeric
1 tsp salt
1 tsp fenugreek leaves
120 g textured soya protein granules
1 tsp garam masala

For serving:
4 tbsp fresh coriander, chopped

Dice the tomatoes and pepper. Peel and finely chop the onions.

In a large saucepan, heat the oil over medium heat and fry the whole spices (cassia and cumin seeds) for 1 minute, then add the onion and fry over low heat for 10 minutes. Add the garlic and ginger pastes, tomato paste and chilli and fry over medium heat for 1 minute.

Add the fresh tomatoes and tomato concassée, the ground spices (except the garam masala) and salt. Mix well and cook, covered, over medium heat for about 5 minutes or until the oil has risen to the surface.

Add the crushed fenugreek leaves, textured soya protein granules and 500 ml of boiling water and cook, covered, over medium heat for 25 minutes, stirring regularly.

Add the garam masala and cook, uncovered, for a further 5 minutes.

Serve sprinkled with the chopped fresh coriander.

Tips

- Enjoy with your choice of flatbread, spiced rice, green chutney (see pp. 146 and 149) or vegetable pickles (see p. 165).
- This *shaak* is also great as a sandwich filling.

કઢી – *Kadhi*

Yoghurt and chickpea-flour soup

***Kadhi* is a yoghurt-based soup, often containing chickpea flour, with different iterations of it found throughout India. While *kadhi* in the Punjab is a rather thick soup topped with onion fritters, the Gujarati version is more liquid and slightly sweeter thanks to the addition of jaggery (see p. 27 for explanations).**

Serves 5
Preparation time: 15 mins
Cooking time: 40 mins

50 g tomatoes (or 30 g tomato concassée)
1 green chilli (optional, see p.16 for tips)
60 g onions
125 g soya yoghurt
30 g chickpea flour
1 tsp salt
½ tsp ground turmeric
3 tbsp neutral cooking oil
½ tsp garlic paste
¼ tsp ground paste
½ tsp fenugreek seeds
¼ tsp black mustard seeds
6 curry leaves
½ tsp jaggery

Dice the tomatoes. Seed and finely chop the chilli. Peel and finely chop the onions.

Mix 450 ml of water, yoghurt, chickpea flour, salt and turmeric until smooth and lump-free.

In a large saucepan, heat 1 tablespoon of the oil over medium-high heat and fry the garlic and ginger pastes for 1 minute before adding the liquid mixture, onion, tomatoes and chilli. Cook over medium heat until it comes to the boil, then reduce the heat to medium-low.

In a small frying pan, heat the 2 remaining tablespoons of oil and fry the whole spices (seeds and curry leaves) for 1 minute. Add the spiced oil and the jaggery to the saucepan and leave to simmer, half-covered, for 5 minutes.

Tips

- Serve with rice with lentils and vegetable pickles.
- For an even more delicious *kadhi*, add 100 ml of coconut milk to the liquid mixture.

Rice

સાદા ચાવલ – *Sada chaval*

Plain basmati rice

In my family, we eat basmati rice almost every day. Even though we often flavour it with spices (see p. 88 for recipe) or coconut milk (see p. 91 for recipe), this particularly aromatic variety of rice can also be enjoyed plain.

Serves 2–3
Preparation time: 5 mins
Cooking time: 15 mins
Resting time: 5 mins

190 g basmati rice
¼ tsp salt

Rinse the rice (see p. 24 for explanations).

Combine the rice, 375 ml of water and salt in a large saucepan or sauté pan and bring to the boil over high heat.

As soon as the water boils, reduce the heat to medium-low and continue cooking, covered, for 12 minutes. Check that the water has evaporated completely and that the rice grains are cooked through. If not, cook for a few minutes longer.

Remove the pan from the heat and leave to rest, covered, for 5 minutes. Carefully lift the lid and fluff the rice with a wide spatula or rice spoon to release as much steam as possible, taking care not to break the grains, and serve immediately.

વઘારેલા ચાવલ – *Vagharela chaval*

Spiced rice

Although it's delicious plain, spiced basmati rice is even tastier. If you've got an extra 5 minutes to spare, I highly recommend you prepare this delicious spiced rice. It's the perfect accompaniment to any vegetable or pulse dish, and is even better when sprinkled with fried onions (see p. 166 for recipe).

Serves 4–6
Preparation time: 10 mins
Cooking time: 20 mins
Resting time: 5 mins

380 g basmati rice
1 tbsp plant-based margarine
½ stick Ceylon cinnamon
3 green cardamom pods
3 cloves
5 black peppercorns
1 black cardamom pod (optional)
¼ tsp salt

Rinse the rice (see p. 24 for explanations).

In a sauté pan that has a lid, melt the margarine over medium heat and fry the spices, uncovered, for 2 minutes.

Pour 30 ml of hot water into the pan and cover the pan immediately to avoid splattering.

After 1 minute, add the rice, 720 ml of boiling water and the salt. Cover and simmer over medium-low heat for 15 minutes. Check that all the water has evaporated and that the rice grains are cooked through. If not, cook for a few minutes longer.

Remove the pan from the heat and leave to rest, covered, for 5 minutes. Carefully lift the lid and fluff the rice with a wide spatula or rice spoon to release as much steam as possible, taking care not to break the grains, and serve immediately.

Tip

As the spices tend to rise to the surface, pick them out just before fluffing the rice to avoid biting into them.

નારયિળ વારા ચાવલ – *Nariyal vara chaval*

Basmati rice with coconut milk

When I make peas or a giant white bean dal with coconut milk, I usually use the remaining coconut milk for my rice. The result is a deliciously fragrant, slightly creamy rice that goes wonderfully well with dal.

Serves 4–6
Preparation time: 5 mins
Cooking time: 15 mins
Resting time: 5 mins

380 g basmati rice
150 ml coconut milk
¼ tsp salt

Rinse the rice (see p. 24 for explanations).

Combine the rice, 600 ml of water, the coconut milk and salt in a large saucepan or sauté pan and bring to the boil over high heat.

As soon as the water boils, reduce the heat to medium-low and continue cooking, covered, for 12 minutes. Check that all the water has evaporated and that the rice grains are cooked through. If not, cook for a few minutes longer.

Remove the pan from the heat and leave to rest, covered, for 5 minutes. Carefully lift the lid and fluff the rice with a wide spatula or rice spoon to release as much steam as possible, taking care not to break the grains, and serve immediately.

ખીચરી – *Khitchri*

Rice with mung beans

Made with rice, a pulse and whole spices, *khitchri* is a particularly tasty and nourishing rice dish that is the perfect accompaniment to any vegetable *shaak*. In my family, we make it using split and hulled mung beans, which have the advantage of cooking in a similar time to rice.

Serves 4
Soaking time: 2 hrs
Preparation time: 10 mins
Cooking time: 20 mins
Resting time: 5 mins

- 100 g mung beans, split and hulled
- 2 green cardamom pods
- 3 black peppercorns
- 3 cloves
- 3 cm cassia bark
- 190 g basmati rice
- 15 g plant-based margarine
- ½ tsp garlic paste
- 1 tbsp fried onions (optional)
- ½ tsp salt

Rinse the mung beans, then soak in plenty of water for 2 hours. Infuse the whole spices in 60 ml of boiling water for 10 minutes.

Rinse the rice (see p. 24 for tips) and the mung beans.

In a sauté pan or large saucepan, melt the margarine over medium heat and fry the garlic paste for 30 seconds, then add the fried onions and fry for 30 seconds.

Remove the pan from the heat, quickly lift the lid and pour the infused water and the spices into the pan. Cover immediately to avoid splattering. Put the pan back on the stove. Over low heat bring the mixture to the boil, then add 500 ml of boiling water, the salt, rice and mung beans.

Bring to the boil over high heat, then reduce the heat to medium-low and cook, covered, for 15 minutes. Check that all the water has evaporated and that the rice grains are cooked through. If not, cook for a few minutes longer.

Remove the pan from the heat and leave to rest, covered, for 5 minutes. Carefully lift the lid and fluff the rice with a wide spatula or rice spoon to release as much steam as possible, taking care not to break the grains, and serve immediately.

Tip

If you don't have split and hulled mung beans, you can use small red or yellow lentils, soaked for 30 minutes.

અક્ની – *Akni*

Rice with vegetables and coconut milk

Like biryani, *akni* is a festive dish that we like to serve on special occasions, but it takes much less time to prepare. We suggest you try it with dried fruit pickles (see p. 162), vegetable pickles (see p. 165), *kachumber* (see p. 145) and a nice glass of lassi (see p. 200).

Serves 6
Preparation time: 20 mins
Cooking time: 1 hr 10 mins

200 g waxy potatoes
80 g carrots
100 g tomatoes
50 g red pepper
80 g onions
3 tbsp neutral cooking oil
2 Indian bay leaves
4 cloves
¼ stick Ceylon cinnamon
2 tsp garlic paste
1 tsp ground coriander
½ tsp ground cumin
¼ tsp ground turmeric
100 g frozen peas (petits pois)
100 ml coconut milk
380 g basmati rice
375 ml coconut cream
1 tbsp fresh coriander, chopped
salt

Peel the potatoes and carrots and cut them into 5-mm thick half moons. Dice the tomatoes. Seed and dice the pepper. Peel and finely chop the onions.

In a large sauté pan, heat the oil over medium heat and fry the whole spices (bay leaves, cloves and cinnamon) for 1 minute, then add the onion and fry over medium-low heat for 5 minutes.

Add the garlic paste and fry for 1 minute over medium-low heat. Add the tomatoes, ground spices and 1 teaspoon of salt and cook for 5 minutes, covered, or until the oil has risen to the surface.

Add the carrots, peas, 100 ml of boiling water and the coconut milk, and leave to cook, covered, over medium heat for 20 minutes. Then add the potatoes and pepper and cook for a further 20 minutes.

Meanwhile, rinse the basmati rice (see p. 24 for tips) and mix 375 ml of boiling water with the coconut cream. Pour into the pan with the rice, ½ teaspoon of salt and the chopped coriander. Mix well, and cook, covered, over medium-low heat for 20 minutes or until the rice is cooked and the liquid has been absorbed. Enjoy!

Tip

You can vary the vegetables you use, but make sure they are fairly firm ones, such as green beans or cauliflower.

પુલાવ – *Poulao*

Rice with vegetables and lentils

A *poulao* is similar to a biryani in the way it is prepared, as it consists of the layers being cooked separately before being assembled and cooked together: *masoor* lentils, mixed vegetables and, of course, rice (see photo on p. 98). Serve with raita (see p. 142), dried fruit pickles and/or vegetables for a complete meal.

Serves 6
Soaking time: 6–12 hrs
Preparation time: 25 mins
Cooking time: 1 hr 30 mins

For the lentils:

100 g *masoor* lentils
½ tsp salt

For the vegetables:

100 g tomatoes
30 g red pepper
175 g carrots
100 g green beans
50 g onions
2 tbsp neutral cooking oil
1 tsp garlic paste
2 tbsp tomato concassée
1 tsp salt
2 tsp ground coriander
1 tsp garam masala
½ tsp ground turmeric

For the rice:

380 g basmati rice
½ tsp salt

For the spice base (*vaghar*):

2 tsp plant-based margarine
2 green cardamom pods
1 black cardamom pod
1 tsp cumin seeds
½ tsp garlic paste

Rinse and soak the lentils in plenty of water for 6–12 hours. Then cook them with the salt in plenty of water until tender (10–15 minutes).

Dice the tomatoes.

Seed the pepper and cut into thin strips. Peel and slice the carrots into thin half moons. Top and tail the green beans and cut into thirds. Peel and finely chop the onion.

In a sauté pan or large saucepan, heat the oil and fry the onion over low heat for about 10 minutes, then add the garlic paste and fry over medium heat for 1 minute. Add the diced fresh tomatoes, tomato concassée, salt and ground spices, and cook, covered, for 5 minutes or until the oil has risen to the surface.

Add the carrot slices and fry for 2 minutes. Pour in 375 ml of boiling water and cook, covered, for 10 minutes before adding the green beans and pepper. Continue cooking for a further 10 minutes.

While the vegetables are cooking, rinse the rice, put it in a saucepan with the salt and cover with plenty of water. Bring to the boil, then precook the rice over medium-high heat for about 5 minutes or until the grains are almost done (but not completely cooked). Drain the rice.

Meanwhile, prepare the spice base (*vaghar*) for the *poulao*: melt the margarine over medium heat in a saucepan large enough to hold the rice, lentils and vegetables. Fry the whole spices for 1 minute, then add the garlic paste and fry for 1 minute. Remove the pan from the heat, quickly lift the lid and pour in 45 ml of boiling water and cover immediately to avoid splattering.

Spread a quarter of the pre-cooked rice over the bottom of the pan and mix with the fried spices. Next, make a layer with half of the lentils, a layer with all the vegetables, the rest of the lentils and finally the rest of the rice. Pour in 375 ml of boiling water, and cook, covered, over medium-low heat for 25 minutes. Serve piping hot.

Tip

You can replace *masoor* lentils with Puy lentils.

લિલોત્રી ની બીરયાની – *Lilotri ni biryani*

Vegetable biryani

Biryani is a festive dish made up of several layers of rice and vegetables, and generously topped with cashew nuts, fresh mint and fried onions for a true burst of flavours (see photo on p. 99). We suggest you try it with *kachumber* (see p. 145) and raita (see p. 142), and a glass of lassi (see p. 200) or masala *tchaas*.

Serves 4
Preparation time: 30 mins
Cooking time: 1 hr 30 mins

For the vegetables:

100 g waxy potatoes
60 g carrots
60 g green beans
50 g tomatoes
35 g red pepper
60 g onions
1 tbsp neutral cooking oil
3 black peppercorns
2 cloves
2 star anise
1 green cardamom pod
1 black cardamom pod
2 cm cassia bark
½ tsp cumin seeds
1 tsp garlic paste
½ tsp salt
1 tsp ground coriander
½ tsp garam masala
¼ tsp ground turmeric
¼ tsp ground cumin
50 g soya yoghurt
15 g fried onions
1 heaped tsp fresh mint leaves, chopped

For the rice:

270 g basmati rice
¾ tsp salt

For the biryani spice base (*vaghar*):

1 heaped tsp plant-based margarine
1 clove
1 green cardamom pod
1 black cardamom pod
1 star anise
½ tsp cumin seeds
¼ stick cinnamon
1 tsp garlic paste
¼ tsp salt

For the topping:

3 tsp raw cashew nuts
1 large red chilli
2 tsp fresh mint leaves, chopped
2 tsp fried onions

Peel and cut the potatoes into 5-mm thick half moons. Peel and slice the carrots into 3-mm slices. Top and tail the green beans and cut into 3-cm lengths. Dice the tomatoes. Seed and cut the pepper into strips. Peel and finely chop the onions.

Fry or roast the potatoes separately.

In a saucepan, heat the oil over medium heat and fry the whole spices for 1 minute, then add the onion and fry over low heat for 10 minutes. Add the garlic paste and fry over medium heat for 30 seconds, then add the tomato, salt and ground spices and cook, covered, for 5 minutes or until the oil has risen to the surface. Add the carrots and cook, covered, for 5 minutes before adding the green beans and pepper.

Cover and cook for a further 15 minutes. Leave the vegetables to cool before mixing with the yoghurt, fried onions and chopped mint.

While the vegetables are cooking, rinse the rice, put it in a saucepan with the salt and cover with plenty of water. Bring to the boil, then precook the rice over medium-high heat for about 5 minutes or until the grains are almost done (but not completely cooked). Drain the rice.

For the topping: brown the cashew nuts in a frying pan for a few minutes.

Wash the chilli and trim the ends.

In a saucepan large enough to hold all the ingredients, melt the margarine over medium heat and fry the whole spices for the spice base for 1 minute, then add the garlic paste and fry for 1 minute. Remove the pan from the heat, quickly lift the lid and pour in 125 ml of water and cover immediately to avoid splattering. Return the pan to the hob over medium heat and bring the mixture to the boil, then boil for about 2 minutes.

Start assembling the biryani: mix a quarter of the rice with the spice base in the bottom of the saucepan, then sprinkle with 1 tsp of fried onions, 1 tsp of cashew nuts and 1 tsp of mint.

Next, make a layer with the vegetables and yoghurt sauce, followed by the potatoes. Add 1 tsp cashew nuts and 1 tsp mint. Add the rest of the rice, then 450 ml of boiling water. Top this last layer with the remaining fried onions and cashew nuts, and place the chilli in the middle.

Cook, covered, over medium-high heat for 5 minutes. Reduce the heat to medium-low and continue cooking for 20 minutes or until the rice is cooked. Serve immediately.

Fried foods

લીલોત્રી ના ભજ્યા – *Lilotri na bhajyia*

Vegetable fritters

Better known by their Hindi name, pakoras, Indian fritters are unique in that they are coated in a spiced batter made with chickpea flour. To make the pastry even crispier, we like to add a little rice flour, but you can use all chickpea flour if you prefer. We recommend filling these fritters with our favourite combination of vegetables – potatoes, onions and peppers – but you can use whichever vegetables you prefer. Just avoid ones that contain a lot of water, such as cauliflower, sweet potato or pumpkin.

Makes about 25 fritters
Preparation time: 25 mins
Cooking time: 15 mins

For the spiced oil:

2 tsp neutral cooking oil
½ tsp black mustard seeds
½ tsp cumin seeds
⅓ stick Ceylon cinnamon
5 curry leaves
1 tsp garlic paste

For the vegetables:

90 g potatoes
25 g red pepper
50 g onions
oil for deep frying

For the batter:

120 g chickpea flour
30 g rice flour
1 tsp ground coriander
½ tsp ground cumin
½ tsp garam masala
½ tsp ground turmeric
1 tsp salt
½ tsp baking powder

In a small saucepan, heat the oil over medium heat and fry the whole spices for 1 minute, then add the garlic paste and fry for 1 minute. Remove the pan from the heat, quickly lift the lid and pour in 125 ml of water and cover immediately to avoid splattering. Return the pan to the hob over medium heat and bring the mixture to the boil. Boil for about 2 minutes then turn off the heat.

Peel the potatoes and cut into 5-mm cubes. Seed and cut the pepper into dice.

Peel and chop the onions.

Combine the dry ingredients (except the baking powder) for the batter, add 200 ml of water little by little and whisk to a thick, smooth and lump-free batter. Stir in the spiced oil (remove the cinnamon stick first), then the vegetables and lastly the baking powder, stirring the batter well before adding each new ingredient.

Prepare a fryer (see p. 32 for tips). When the oil is hot enough, drop in 1 tablespoon of batter-coated vegetables at a time. Space the fritters about 2 cm apart and fry until golden brown underneath. Then, turn them over and fry for a further minute or so, until the fritters are evenly golden brown.

Place the fritters on a plate lined with kitchen paper and repeat the process until all the batter has been used up.

Tip

Serve with *kachumber* (see p. 145), green chutney (see pp. 146 and 149) or a date and tamarind chutney (see p. 151).

બટેટા વડા – *Bateta vada*

Potato croquettes

Bateta vada **are fried dumplings made with mashed potatoes, deliciously flavoured with coconut and coated in a spicy, crispy batter. Served with a green chutney with coconut milk (see p. 146), chilli chutney or date and tamarind chutney (see p. 151), they'll be the stars of your snack repertoire!**

Makes 18 croquettes
Preparation time: 15 mins
Cooking time: 40 mins

For the mashed potatoes:
400 g waxy potatoes
2 tbsp dessicated coconut
2 tbsp fresh coriander, chopped
1 tsp white sesame seeds
1 tsp ground coriander
1 tsp garam masala
½ tsp ground cumin
¼ tsp ground turmeric
½ tsp ground cinnamon
½ tsp salt

For the batter:
1 tsp neutral cooking oil
1 tsp mustard seeds
10 curry leaves
60 g chickpea flour
15 g rice flour
1 tsp ground turmeric

oil for deep-frying

Brush the skins of the potatoes to remove any dirt and rinse. Cut 3 or 4 slits in the skin lengthways (this makes it easier to peel them later) and steam until cooked through, about 20 minutes.

In a small frying pan, heat the neutral oil over medium heat and fry the whole spices for the batter for 1 minute.

In a bowl, combine the flours with 100 ml of water and the turmeric, mixing until smooth. Add the spiced oil.

When the potatoes are done, peel while still warm, then mash them and stir in all the other ingredients for the mashed potatoes.

Divide the dough into 18 balls weighing around 25 g each. Prepare a fryer (see p. 32 for tips). Dip a few of the croquettes in the batter.

When the oil is hot enough, put the croquettes coated in the batter into the oil about 2 cm apart and fry until golden brown underneath. Then, turn them over and fry for a further 1 minute or so, until the fritters are evenly golden brown.

Place the croquettes on a plate lined with kitchen paper and repeat the process until all the croquettes have been coated and fried.

Tips

- Using rice flour will make the croquettes crispier. If you don't have rice flour, simply use the equivalent amount of chickpea flour.
- Cooking times vary according to the size of the potatoes, so use medium-sized potatoes of a similar size, or cut them into even pieces if necessary.

દાળ ના ભજ્યા – *dal na bhajyia*

Lentil fritters

For the *shaak* recipe (see p. 71), we use whole mung beans. Here, however, we use split and hulled ones that are small, oval and yellow. Of all the fritter recipes in this book, these are definitely the easiest and quickest to make. But you still need to soak the mung beans for 24 hours.

Makes about 20 fritters
Soaking time: 24 hrs
Preparation time: 20 mins
Cooking time: 5 mins

250 g split, hulled mung beans
100 g onions
15 g garlic
10 g fresh ginger
1 green chilli (optional)
2 tbsp fresh coriander, chopped
2 tbsp fresh mint leaves, chopped
2 tsp ground coriander
1 tsp ground cumin
1 tsp ground turmeric
1 tsp garam masala
½ tsp ground cinnamon
½ tsp salt
¼ tsp bicarbonate of soda

oil for deep-frying

Rinse the beans three or four times until the water runs clear, then leave to soak in plenty of water for 24 hours. After 12 hours, drain and rinse them, then soak again for 12 hours, before draining and rinsing them one last time.

Peel and chop the onion, garlic and ginger. Finely chop the chilli.

In a food processor fitted with an S-blade, place the well-drained beans and the rest of the ingredients, except for the bicarbonate of soda. Using the 'pulse' button, gradually whiz all the ingredients together to an evenly chunky consistency. All the ingredients should be the same size and should be easy to shape into patties. Add the bicarbonate of soda to the mixture.

In a frying pan or sauté pan, heat a 2-cm layer of oil (there should be enough oil for the fritters to be half-submerged) over medium-high heat.

Use your hands to shape about 20 small, smooth patties about 1 cm thick.

When the oil is hot enough (see p. 32 for tips), put the fritters into the oil 2 cm apart. As soon as the edges of the fritters start to brown (after about 2 minutes), turn them over and continue frying for a further 2 minutes or until completely golden brown.

As each fritter is done, place it on a plate lined with kitchen paper.

Tips

To make shaping the fritters easier, lightly oil your hands, as the mixture is a little sticky.
– Serve with a green chutney with coconut milk (see p. 146), chilli chutney or a date and tamarind chutney (see p. 151).

પેટીસ – *Pétisses*

Potato fritters stuffed with textured soya protein

Pétisses are fritters usually filled with a generous minced meat-based stuffing. Here, we have substituted the meat with textured soya protein. It takes almost an hour to prepare these fritters as various stages are involved, but if you have a team of helpers to shape and stuff them, the process will be quicker.

Makes 10 fritters
Soaking time: 25 mins
Preparation time: 30 mins
Cooking time: 5 mins

For textured soya protein:

50 g textured soya protein granules
½ tsp ground cumin
½ tsp ground coriander
½ tsp garam masala
½ tsp ground turmeric
¼ tsp salt

For the pureed potatoes:

400 g waxy potatoes
½ tsp salt
½ tsp ground turmeric

For the stuffing:

50 g tomatoes
50 g onions
1 small chilli (optional, see p.16 for tips)
1 tsp neutral cooking oil
½ tsp garlic paste
½ tsp ginger paste
½ tsp ground cumin
⅛ tsp ground cinnamon
¼ tsp salt
fine breadcrumbs
oil for deep frying

In a small saucepan, combine all the ingredients for the textured soya protein with 250 ml of boiling water. Cover and leave to stand for about 25 minutes or until the soya protein granules have softened and absorbed as much of the marinade as they can. Drain off as much of the remaining liquid as possible by placing the granules in a fine mesh strainer and pressing down with a large spoon or fork.

Brush the skins of the potatoes to remove any dirt and rinse. Cut 3 or 4 slits in the skin lengthways (this makes it easier to peel them later) and steam until they are cooked through, about 20 minutes. Peel while still warm, puree them and mix in the salt and turmeric.

To make the stuffing, finely dice the tomatoes, and peel and finely chop the onions and chilli.

Heat the oil in a frying pan over medium heat and fry the garlic and ginger pastes for 1 minute, then add the cumin, cinnamon and salt and fry for 30 seconds. Stir in the soya protein granules and fry for 5 minutes, stirring regularly. Transfer the contents of the pan to a bowl and mix in the onion, tomato and chilli.

Divide the potato puree into 20 equal portions, shape into 20 balls and gently flatten them between your hands to make discs about 3 mm thick.

Place a generous amount of stuffing (about 2 teaspoons) on top of 10 of the discs, leaving a space of about 3-4 mm around the edge. Place a second patty on top of the stuffing. Use your fingers to seal the two discs to form nice smooth patties, then coat each patty with breadcrumbs.

In a frying pan or sauté pan, heat 2–3 cm of oil (there should be enough oil for the patties to be half submerged) over medium-high heat. When the oil is hot enough (see p. 32 for tips), put the patties into the oil, spacing them 3 cm apart. When the edges of the patties start to brown (after about 2 minutes), turn them over and continue frying for a further 2 minutes or until golden brown.

As each fritter is done, place it on a plate lined with kitchen paper.

Tips

- Serve with *kachumber* (see p. 145), vegetable pickles, a green chutney (see pp. 146 and 149) or date and tamarind chutney (see p. 151) and a squeeze of lemon.
- These *pétisses* will keep in an airtight container in the fridge for up to 3 days. Reheat them in the oven.

સમોસા ના પડ – *Samosa na par*

Samosa pastry sheets

As well as selling pizzas from his food truck every evening, my uncle also sold samosas, which were what made him famous. My aunt was in charge of preparing the dough for the pizzas and samosas, as well as the toppings, and I remember the Wednesdays I spent as a child watching her work with incredible speed and agility, putting everything together. It wasn't until I wanted to learn how to make my own samosas that I truly appreciated the skill and dexterity of her technique, and began to value these crispy little triangles! I should warn you that making samosa pastry sheets requires time, motivation and precision. However, here are all my tips and advice on how to get it right on your very first go!

Makes 30 small samosas
Preparation time: 30 mins
Resting time: 45 mins
Cooking time: 30 mins

180 g white T45 wheat flour + a little extra for shaping

¾ tsp salt

½ tbsp neutral cooking oil + a little extra for shaping

In a wide, shallow bowl (such as a salad bowl), combine the flour, salt and oil with your fingertips. Gradually add 90 ml of warm water while combining the water and flour with your fingertips. Firstly, add the water in amounts of about 1 tablespoon at a time until the dough can be shaped into a ball. When the dough becomes very moist, add 1 teaspoon of water at a time while continuing to knead.

Once all the water has been absorbed, knead the dough for 10 minutes, then shape into a ball. Leave the dough to rest in the bowl, covered with a clean damp tea towel, for 45 minutes.

Weigh the smooth, supple resulting ball of dough and divide into 15 equal portions. Shape into 15 balls and flatten them into round patties. Put them back into the bowl and cover with the tea towel again to prevent them from drying out.

Take a dough patty, dust it with flour and use a rolling pin to roll it out into a disc about 10–11 cm in diameter. Repeat the operation with a second disc.

Using your fingers, spread a thin layer of oil over one of the discs, making sure you don't miss even a millimetre, then dust it with flour before placing the second disc on top. Dust the worktop with flour and also dust the top of the two discs on top of each other, then roll out the dough into a disc about 17-18 cm in diameter, so that you have a double sheet of samosa dough.

↓

Heat a non-stick frying pan over high heat. Once the pan is hot, turn the heat down to medium-low. Place the double sheet of dough in the pan and cook for 30 seconds before turning it over and cooking the other side for a further 30 seconds. Immediately remove the dough and gently peel the two sheets apart.

They should be supple and just pre-cooked. As you go along, place the separated sheets on a plate covered with a tea towel.

Once all the sheets have been cooked and separated, place them on top of each other and, using a sharp knife, cut off about 1.5 cm from the left-hand side and 1.5 cm from the right-hand side, to obtain a wide 'rectangular' strip with straight sides and rounded top and bottom edges.

Then cut the pile of sheets in half lengthways, down the middle. You will have 32 sheets of samosa dough with two long straight edges and two short rounded edges.

Tips

- Pre-cooked, these sheets can be stored stacked for up to 2 days in the fridge, wrapped in a damp tea towel, then in an airtight bag, or for up to 2 months in the freezer, in an airtight bag.
- Don't throw away the dough scraps! Fry them and serve as a snack with date and tamarind chutney (see p. 151).
- If you have trouble separating the two sheets, there are several possible reasons why: you didn't put enough oil or enough flour between the two discs, or you overcooked the dough – reduce the heat and/or cooking time if necessary.

લીલોતરી ના સમોસા – *Lilotri na samosa*

Vegetable samosas

Originating in Central Asia and the Middle East, these triangular fritters are now eaten throughout India. Made with different types of doughs and fillings, they come in various sizes and with a range of accompaniments. In my family, we make samosas with very thin dough, which is traditionally filled with minced meat, vegetables or pulses (see p. 121 for recipe). Samosas are the stars of both Indian street food and for celebrations. We enjoy them on special occasions as a snack or starter, served with pickles, chutneys and a good chai.

Makes 30 small samosas
Preparation time: 1 hr
Resting time: 1 hr
Cooking time: 1 hr 15 mins

30 sheets samosa dough (see p. 113 for recipe)
7½ tsp white wheat flour for the 'glue'
oil for deep frying

For the filling:
400 g potatoes
100 g carrots
100 g frozen peas (petits pois)
1 tsp neutral cooking oil
1 tsp black mustard seeds
1 tsp cumin seeds
1 tsp garlic paste
½ tsp ground cumin
½ tsp ground cardamom
½ tsp ground turmeric
salt

For the filling: Peel the potatoes and carrots and cut them into cubes measuring about 5 mm.

Place the three vegetables in a saucepan with ½ teaspoon of salt and cover with water.

Bring to the boil over high heat, then reduce the heat to medium-high and cook for 10 minutes. Drain.

Heat the oil in a saucepan over medium heat and fry the seeds for 1 minute, add the garlic paste, ground spices and ¼ teaspoons of salt and fry for 1 minute. Stir in the vegetables and fry over low heat, covered, for 5 minutes. Add 1 or 2 teaspoons of water if the mixture begins to stick to the bottom of the pan. Spread the vegetables on a plate to cool completely.

Prepare the samosa 'glue'. Use a small whisk to mix the flour and 10 teaspoons of water to a smooth and lump-free liquid.

Take a sheet of samosa dough and place the shortest side closest to you, with the shorter of the two longer sides to your left.

Where the straight side starts on the left just above the curve, count about 3 cm up and make a tiny nick in the dough with the tip of a knife. Lift the bottom left corner and fold it over to the right at the height of the nick in the dough, where an almost right angle should form at the height of the nick.

Apply a 1-cm wide strip of glue along the left-hand side. Wipe your fingers clean after applying each strip of glue to avoid getting any on the outside of the samosa.

Fold the bottom edge over the left edge and press lightly to glue them together.

You now have a cone that is ready to be filled.

Place 1 tablespoon of filling in the cone and press down well with your fingertips. There should be 5 mm of space above the filling. If there is more, add a little more filling and press it down again.

Apply the glue all over the inside of the part to be folded, including the corners.

Start by sealing the corners well, then fold the piece of pastry with the glue over to close the samosa. It is important that the samosa is completely sealed to prevent the frying oil from getting inside.

Place the samosas on a plate, covered with a clean tea towel. Cover with cling film and leave to rest in the fridge for 1 hour. This resting time helps to reduce the appearance of bubbles on the samosas as they cook.

Get a saucepan ready and heat it over medium-high heat. Pour in 3–4 cm of oil so that the samosas will be completely submerged (see p. 32 for tips). When the oil is hot enough, reduce the heat to medium and immediately put in as many samosas as possible, but without overcrowding them. Gently hold the samosas down in the oil for the first minute, then fry each side for 5 minutes. Just before removing the samosas, turn up the heat again.

Place the golden brown samosas on a plate lined with kitchen paper. Wait 1 minute for the oil to heat up again, then reduce the heat to medium again and fry the remaining samosas.

Tips

Folding: if the 15 discs of dough are not all exactly the same size, the pieces will vary in shape, and this will inevitably affect the folding process. That's why I recommend folding each sheet completely first, without any glue or filling, to ensure your triangles are the right shape and can be properly sealed.

Cooking: although the frying should be over medium heat (or even slightly higher), it is important that the samosas are immersed in very hot oil. That's why it's important to turn up the heat between each batch to ensure you get nice, golden, crispy samosas.

Save time: as making samosas is very time-consuming, you can save time by preparing the dough and the filling in advance, but also by using a tinned or frozen mix of vegetables. Once they have been stuffed, you can keep the samosas in the fridge, covered with cling film to prevent them drying out, for 2 days before frying them. You can also freeze stuffed samosas for up to 2 months and fry them straight out of the freezer.
Fried samosas can be stored in an airtight container in the fridge then heated up in the oven for a few minutes. Frozen fried samosas – which keep for up to 2 months in the freezer – should be defrosted in the fridge for 24 hours and then reheated in the oven.

મગ ની દાળ ના સમોસા – *Mug ni dal na samosa*

Mung bean samosas

As with the lentil fritters, this samosa recipe uses hulled mung beans, which are a type of pulse that cooks quickly. Of the three fillings that my family makes (minced beef, vegetables or lentils), this has always been my favourite – the combination of the soft lentils and the crispy shell is so satisfying.

Makes 30 small samosas
Soaking time: 2 hrs
Preparation time: 10 mins
Cooking time: 20 mins
Resting time: 1 hr 30 mins

7½ tsp white wheat flour for the 'glue'
30 sheets samosa dough (see p. 113 for recipe)
oil for deep frying

For the filling:

200 g mung beans, split and hulled
1 tsp neutral cooking oil
1 tsp cumin seeds
10 curry leaves
1 tsp garlic paste
1 tsp ground coriander
½ tsp ground cumin
½ tsp ground cinnamon
¼ tsp ground turmeric
¼ tsp salt
40 g yellow onions
1 green or red chilli (optional)
5 tbsp fresh coriander, chopped

For the filling: Rinse the mung beans and leave to soak in plenty of water for 2 hours. Rinse and drain well.

Heat the oil in a saucepan over medium heat and fry the cumin seeds and curry leaves for 1 minute, then add the garlic paste, spices and salt and fry for 30 seconds.

Stir in the mung beans and fry for 2 minutes before adding 250 ml of boiling water. Partially cover the pan and cook for 15 minutes over medium-low heat, until all the water has been absorbed and the mung beans are cooked through but still whole – they should not be mushy. If they still seem hard by the time all the water has been absorbed, add a few spoonfuls of water and continue cooking a few minutes longer. If they are done before the water has been completely absorbed, simply drain off any excess water at the end of cooking. The beans will finish cooking when the samosas are fried.

Spread the spiced beans out on a large plate and leave to cool completely.

Peel and finely chop the onion. Finely chop the chilli. Mix well with the chopped fresh coriander and the cooled beans.

Stuff the samosas with the filling and fry them following the steps in the recipe for vegetable samosas (see p. 116).

Tips

- This filling can be prepared 3 days in advance, stored in the fridge in an airtight container.
- If you don't have time to prepare your own sheets of samosa dough, you can use this filling to stuff turnovers using shop-bought plant-based puff pastry.

Flatbreads

રોટલી – *Rotli*

Chapatis

Also known as rotis or *rotlis* depending on the region, chapatis are a staple food eaten at almost every meal. Although my mother didn't make chapatis, my aunt and cousins regularly brought them to us, and it was my cousins Zehra and Iliasse who taught me how to prepare them. When I was a child, and lucky enough to be at my aunt's house while she was making them, I loved eating them hot and rolled up like a pancake, drizzled with ghee (clarified butter) and sugar. Traditionally, we eat them with *shaaks* and dals.

Makes 12 chapatis
Preparation time: 30 mins
Resting time: 1 hr
Cooking time: 30 mins

300 g *atta* flour + a little extra for the worktop

½ tsp salt

1 tsp neutral cooking oil

plant-based margarine

In a wide, shallow bowl, combine the flour, salt and oil with your fingertips. Add 250 ml of lukewarm water, a little at a time, mixing by hand until the dough is smooth. Firstly, add the water in amounts of about 1 tablespoon at a time until the dough can be shaped into a ball. When the dough starts to become very moist, add 1 teaspoon of water at a time while continuing to knead.

Once all the water has been absorbed, knead the dough for a good 10 minutes until it forms a soft ball that is no longer sticky. Leave the dough to rest in the bowl, covered with a clean damp tea towel, for 1 hour.

Knead the dough again for a few minutes, shape into a sausage and cut into 12 equal pieces. Flatten the resulting pieces into flattish balls, put them back in the bowl and cover with the tea towel to prevent them drying out.

Put enough flour in a bowl to dip each ball of dough in before rolling it out.

Using a rolling pin, roll out the first ball of dough into a disc about 15 cm in diameter and about 1 mm thick. If the dough sticks to the worktop and the rolling pin, add a little flour, but try to add as little as possible.

Heat a large non-stick frying pan over medium heat and melt the margarine in a separate pan. Remove as much flour as possible from the surface of each chapati by tossing it quickly from one hand to the other, then place it in the hot pan and turn it over as soon as the first bubbles appear. Leave to cook for 30 seconds, or as long as it takes for brown spots to appear on the surface, then turn it over again. Continue cooking for 30 seconds, gently pressing down on the chapati, turning it clockwise with a clean, dry tea towel (this will stop you from burning your fingertips). The chapati should swell up.

Remove the chapati from the pan and brush the top with melted margarine before cooking the next one.

Wrap the chapatis as you go in a clean tea towel and place them under an upside-down soup plate to keep them nice and warm and avoid them drying out.

Tip

Chapatis will keep for 3 days wrapped in aluminium foil or a thin cotton tea towel at room temperature or in the fridge, or for 3 months in the freezer.

नान – *Naan*

Naan

For a long time I thought it was difficult to make naan as soft and toasted as they are in restaurants where they are made in a tandoor, the traditional Indian oven in which these delicious breads are usually baked. Although you can't get the characteristic flavour of naan baked in a tandoor at home, a simple frying pan with a lid can produce naans that are just as soft and tasty, with lovely brown bubbles. Naans are the perfect accompaniment to any dish with a sauce, but I also like to use them as you would sandwich bread, folded in half and filled with raita (see p. 142) or *kachumber* (see p. 145), tandoori tofu (see p. 76), vegetable pickles and raw vegetables.

Makes 8 naans
Preparation time: 30 mins
Resting time: 2 hrs
Cooking time: 10 mins

- 13 g fresh baker's yeast
- 1 tsp sugar
- 260 g white wheat flour (T45) + a little extra for the worktop
- ¼ tsp bicarbonate of soda
- ¼ tsp baking powder
- ½ tsp salt
- 50 g soya yoghurt
- 2 tsp neutral cooking oil + a little extra for shaping
- 4 tbsp plant-based margarine
- 1 tsp garlic paste (optional)
- 8 tsp fresh parsley or coriander, chopped
- 4 tsp nigella seeds (optional)
- fleur de sel

Crumble the fresh baker's yeast, mix with 120 ml of warm water and the sugar, then leave to stand for around 10 minutes.

In a wide, shallow bowl (such as a salad bowl), combine the flour, bicarbonate of soda, baking powder and salt. Add the yoghurt and oil to the rehydrated baker's yeast, then pour this mixture over the flour, stirring with a large wooden spoon until all the liquid has been absorbed.

Oil your hands and work the dough into a smooth ball and knead for around 10 minutes. As the dough is sticky, you can oil your hands throughout the kneading process.

Coat the ball of dough with a little oil and leave it to rest in the bowl, covered with a clean tea towel, in a warm, dry place away from draughts, for an hour and a half to 2 hours, until the dough has doubled in size.

Knock back the dough, shape it into a ball, divide it into 8 pieces and place them on a large floured plate or tray, a few centimetres apart and covered with the tea towel. Leave to rest for about 10 minutes.

Meanwhile, melt the margarine and mix with the garlic paste, if using.

Using a rolling pin, roll out the first piece of dough to form an oval shape approximately 2–3 mm thick. Roll out the dough from the middle outwards, rather than from top to bottom, to avoid the naan sticking to the worktop or the rolling pin and having to add more flour.

Sprinkle one side of the naan with fresh herbs and/or nigella seeds and roll lightly with the rolling pin so that they stick to the dough.

Heat a large non-stick frying pan over medium-high heat. Place the naan, topping side up, in the hot pan and cook, covered, until several bubbles form on the surface (about 1 minute). Turn the naan over, cover again and continue cooking for about 1 minute.

Place the naans on a plate as you go, brushing them immediately with melted plain or garlic margarine. Sprinkle with a little fleur de sel and cover with a clean tea towel.

Tips

- You can replace the fresh yeast with 4.5 g of dried baker's yeast.
- When it's not particularly hot, I leave the dough to rise in a turned-off oven but with the oven light on. The light heats the oven enough (but not too much!) to create an atmosphere in which the dough will rise.
- Although you can omit the toppings, I would advise against not brushing the surface with the melted margarine and sprinkling with fleur de sel, as these enhance both the texture and flavour of the naans.
- Naans are best eaten as soon as they're made, but you can store them, wrapped in a clean tea towel and in an airtight container, for up to 24 hours. They can also be frozen. They reheat very well in a toaster or frying pan.

લછછા પરાઠા – *Laccha paratha*

Laccha parathas

Whether round, square or triangular, *laccha* parathas all have the distinctive feature of being flatbreads made of thin layers separated by vegetable oil, rather like puff pastry. Richer than chapatis and taking a little longer to prepare, they can be eaten simply with raita (see p. 142), chutney or pickles. They can also be served with any vegetable or pulse dish.

Makes 8 parathas
Preparation time: 30 mins
Resting time: 30 mins
Cooking time: 40 mins

300 g *atta* flour + a little extra for shaping
1 tsp salt
neutral cooking oil

Place the flour in a wide, shallow bowl, then mix in the salt and 3 teaspoons of cooking oil, using your fingertips. Gradually add 250 ml warm water, mixing by hand until the dough is nice and smooth. On a floured worktop or in the bowl, knead the dough for at least 10 minutes until it forms a soft, non-sticky ball.

Brush the dough with oil, cover with a clean damp tea towel and leave to rest in the bowl for 30 minutes.

Knead the dough again for a few minutes, shape it into a ball, divide it into 8 pieces, flatten them into round flattish balls and cover them with the damp tea towel.

Prepare a small bowl of flour (about 100 g), a small bowl of oil (about 80 ml) and a pastry brush, a plate and a clean tea towel on which to place the cooked parathas.

Take the first piece of dough and dust it with flour. Using a rolling pin, roll out the dough into a disc about 12 cm in diameter (dust with flour if the dough starts to stick to the worktop or the rolling pin). Using your fingertips, spread some oil over the entire surface of the disc, then sprinkle it with a few pinches of flour.

Fold the dough into pleats as if making a fan or roll it up like a crepe, pressing down firmly.

↓

Fold the dough like a fan or roll it like a pancake, tightly.

Roll the resulting strip of dough into a snail-like shell, keeping it tight.

Fold the outer end of the roll over the centre and press it in.

Dust the resulting roll in flour, then roll out into a disc about 12 cm in diameter. Remove as much flour as possible from the surface of each paratha by tossing it quickly from one hand to the other.

Heat a non-stick frying pan over medium heat. Oil the hot pan and put in the first paratha. Cook for about 1 minute, until the first bubbles appear. Oil the top of the paratha before turning it over with a spatula, then cook for about 2 minutes. Turn the paratha over again and continue cooking for 1 minute. Finally, turn the paratha over three or four times every 15 seconds, until you have nice golden brown spots on both sides.

Oil the pan again and repeat the process until all the dough has been used up. Wrap the cooked parathas in a clean tea towel as you go. This stops them from drying out and keeps them nice and hot.

Tips

- The amount of water may vary from one brand of flour to another. For this reason, the water must be added gradually (starting with 50 ml, then adding 1 teaspoon at a time as soon as the dough starts to come together). Do not stop adding water even when the dough comes together, as it must be sufficiently moist to produce soft parathas.
Throughout the cooking process, and as the bubbles appear, gently press down on the paratha while turning it clockwise, so that it cooks evenly and stays soft.
- If there's any flour residue in the pan, remove it before cooking the next paratha.
- Parathas can be kept in the fridge for about 4 days wrapped – when cool – in a clean tea towel, then in a plastic bag or in an airtight container. You can also freeze them.
- Reheat them for a few minutes in a lightly oiled pan or in the oven.

બટેટા એને તોફુ ના પરાઠા – *Bateta ane tofu na paratha*

Potato and tofu parathas

Stuffed parathas offer a host of possibilities and can form the basis of a very nourishing and satisfying meal. Parathas are usually served with yoghurt, pickles and chutneys. Very popular with those who like a savoury breakfast, they are also ideal as a snack or as part of a packed lunch. I like to add grated tofu to the traditional potato stuffing, as it is high in protein and adds a little chewiness. I also add toasted sesame seeds for crunch.

Makes 8 parathas
Preparation time: 30 mins
Resting time: 1 hr
Cooking time: 1 hr 30 mins

For the dough:

300 g *atta* flour + a little extra for shaping
1 tsp salt
neutral cooking oil

For the filling:

200 g firm plain tofu
400 g potatoes, waxy or floury
75 g onions
1 small fresh chilli (optional, see p.16 for tips)
4 tbsp fresh coriander
6 tsp white sesame seeds
2 tsp ground coriander
1 tsp ground cumin
½ tsp garam masala
¼ tsp ground turmeric
½ tsp salt

Place the flour in a wide, shallow bowl, then mix in the salt and 3 teaspoons of cooking oil, using your fingertips. Gradually add 250 ml of lukewarm water, mixing with your hands until the dough is smooth. On a floured worktop or in the bowl, knead the dough for at least 10 minutes until it forms a soft, non-sticky ball.

Brush the dough with oil, cover with a clean damp tea towel and leave to rest in the bowl for 30 minutes.

Drain the tofu for 30 minutes (see p. 26 for tips). Brush the skins of the potatoes to remove any dirt and rinse. Cut 3 or 4 slits in the skin lengthways (this makes it easier to peel them later) and steam until cooked through, about 20 minutes.

Peel the onions and finely chop them. Finely chop the chilli and the coriander. Peel the potatoes while still warm, and grate them, along with the tofu.

Toast the sesame seeds in a small frying pan over medium-high heat for about 2 minutes, stirring constantly. Set aside the golden brown seeds.

In a small mixing bowl, combine the ground spices and the salt. In a medium bowl, mix the grated potatoes, grated tofu, salt-spice mixture, coriander and fresh chilli until smooth. Weigh the filling, divide it into 8 equal portions and shape into 8 compact balls.

Take a ball of dough, dust it with flour, then roll it out into a disc 14–15 cm in diameter. If the dough sticks to the worktop and the rolling pin, dust with flour, but use as little as possible.

Place a ball of filling in the middle of a disc. Enclose the filling by lifting two opposite sides of the dough and pinching them together hard enough to seal them just above the filling.

Do the same with the other two sides of the disc. Then, seal and fold the four remaining openings over the filling and gently flatten the paratha between your hands. Dust with flour and roll it out into a disc 17–18 cm in diameter. Remove as much flour as possible from both sides of the paratha, tossing it quickly and gently from one hand to the other.

Heat a non-stick frying pan slightly above medium heat. Oil one side of the paratha, put into the hot pan and cook for 3 minutes. Oil the top side, turn the paratha over and cook for a further 3 minutes. Then turn the paratha over to cook for 30 seconds on each side again.

Oil the pan again and repeat the process until all the dough has been used up. Wrap the cooked parathas in a clean tea towel as you go. This stops them from drying out and keeps them nice and hot.

To save time, roll a new ball as soon as you put one paratha in the pan.

Tips

- Parathas can be kept in the fridge for about 3 days wrapped – when cool – in a clean tea towel, then in a plastic bag or in an airtight container.
- You can also freeze them.
- Reheat them for a few minutes in a lightly oiled pan or in the oven.
- Before cooking them, avoid placing the stuffed parathas one on top of the other, but if you do, make sure to separate them with a sheet of baking paper and then cover them with a damp tea towel until you're ready to cook them.

પુરી – *Pouri*

Puris

Puris are little fried breads that are very quick to prepare. To ensure the puris are puffed and not soggy with oil, do not overwork the dough or leave it to rest for longer than a few minutes. These breads are particularly good with potato *shaak* (see p. 41) or even *khir* (see p. 178), but they are just as delicious with any *shaak* or dal. As a general rule, I would recommend eating them either piping hot or within an hour of cooking, to avoid them deflating and drying out.

Makes 12 puris
Preparation time: 20 mins
Resting time: 5 mins
Cooking time: 15 mins

300 g *atta* flour + a little extra for shaping

½ tsp salt

2 tsp neutral cooking oil

oil for deep frying

In a wide, shallow bowl, mix the flour, salt and 1½ teaspoons of oil with your fingertips.

Gradually add about 180 ml of water, mixing by hand until you have a firm, non-sticky ball of dough. Add ½ teaspoon of oil and work the dough briefly into a smooth ball. Leave the dough to rest for 5 minutes under a clean tea towel.

Divide the dough into 12 balls and flatten each one between your hands to form a small round patty. Cover them with the tea towel you used previously.

Prepare the fryer (see p. 32 for tips) by pouring in oil to a depth of around 5 cm – there should be enough oil to completely cover the puris, which will swell during cooking.

Roll out the first patty into a disc about 10 cm in diameter and 1–2 mm thick. If the dough sticks to the worktop or the rolling pin too much, dust with a little flour, but make sure you remove as much as possible from the surface of the puris before frying them.

When the oil is hot, put in a puri and, as soon as it rises to the surface, press down lightly with a skimmer or spider strainer to submerge it completely so that it puffs up. Then turn the puri over three times until golden brown on both sides.

Place the fried puris onto a plate lined with kitchen paper, and avoid overlapping them so that they don't deflate.

CONDIMENTS

રાયતા – *Raita*

Raita

Raita is a condiment made with yoghurt, spices and raw vegetables, but the ingredients vary considerably from one family to the next and one region of India to another. In my family, we usually prepare it with cucumber and toasted cumin, but sometimes with grated carrots and apples. As yoghurt is quite refreshing, it's a particularly popular condiment with spicy dishes.

Makes 1 medium bowl
Preparation time: 5 mins

200 g cucumber
200 g plain soya yoghurt
½ tsp toasted ground cumin
¼ tsp salt
1 tbsp fresh coriander, chopped
1 tbsp fresh mint leaves, chopped

Peel and seed the cucumber, then chop finely.

In a bowl, mix together the yoghurt, cumin, salt, fresh herbs and cucumber.

Keep up to 48 hrs in the fridge until ready to use.

Tips

- Serve with biryani or rice with vegetables and coconut milk.
- If you prefer, replace the cucumber with thin slices of radish or grated carrots, or make a mixture of two or three raw vegetables.
- If you don't have any toasted cumin, you can use regular ground cumin.

કચુમ્બર – *Kachumber*

Lemony tomatoes with spring onions

Although often described as a salad, *kachumber* is usually served as a condiment, like a chutney or pickle. However, it's much more refreshing as it is made with raw vegetables. It is the perfect accompaniment to all kinds of fritters and can also be served with biryani (see p. 100). In a much less conventional way, it can also be eaten on bruschetta-style toast with an aperitif.

Makes 12 portions (served as a condiment)
Preparation time: 15 mins
Chilling time: 1 hr

225 g juicy tomatoes
55 g spring onions
100 g shallots
10 mint leaves
3 medium radishes (optional)
¼ tsp sugar
¼ tsp grated ginger
2 tbsp lemon juice
½ tsp salt
1 tbsp white vinegar

Finely dice the tomatoes. Finely chop the spring onions, peel and finely chop the shallots and mint. Cut the radishes into thin slices.

Mix all the ingredients in a bowl.

Leave the *kachumber* in the fridge for at least 1 hour before serving to allow all the flavours to marry.

Tips

- *Kachumber* can be stored in an airtight jar for up to 3 days in the fridge.
- If you wish to use *kachumber* as a bruschetta topping, halve the amount of lemon juice and omit the vinegar.

નારિયેળ ની લીલી ચટણી – *Naryel ni lili chutni*

Green chutney with coconut milk

This bright green chutney brings together the freshness of mint and coriander with the sweetness of coconut and peanuts. It is usually served with fritters, but also with stuffed parathas (see p. 136). As it tends to solidify in the fridge, we recommend taking out the required quantity 30 minutes before serving to restore its creamy texture.

Makes 1 large jar
Preparation time: 15 mins

100 g green pepper
1 green chilli
100 g fresh coriander
50 g fresh mint leaves
10 g fresh ginger
5 g garlic
30 g dessicated coconut
35 g roasted peanuts unsalted
100 ml coconut milk
1 tbsp olive oil
1 tsp lemon juice
1 tsp salt

Seed and cut the green pepper into 3 pieces. Remove the stalks and cut the chilli into 3 equal pieces. Chop the coriander (including the stems if they are tender) and mint. Peel the ginger and garlic and chop into small pieces.

Whiz all the ingredients together to a smooth paste.

Store in an airtight jar in the fridge.

Tip

This chutney can be kept for up to 5 days in the fridge or 3 months in the freezer.

તીખી લીલી ચટણી – *Tikhi lili chutni*

Green chilli chutney

Here's another bright green chutney, but much less sweet than the coconut milk chutney! This recipe will appeal more to those chilli lovers, and will spice up your fritters, parathas and even your sandwiches.

Makes 1 jar
Preparation time: 15 mins

3 green chillies (your choice of variety, depending on how much heat you can take, see p.16 for tips)
40 g onions
1 bunch fresh coriander
1 bunch fresh mint
10 g fresh ginger
5 g garlic
¼ tsp salt
¼ tsp ground cumin
½ lemon, juiced

Remove the stalks and chop the chillies. Peel and chop the onion. Chop the coriander (including the stems if tender) and the mint leaves. Peel the ginger and garlic.

Put all the ingredients in a food processor fitted with an S-blade and whiz until the chutney is smooth. If it's very thick, add a few spoonfuls of water or half a tomato.

Tip

Store in an airtight jar in the fridge for up to 5 days or up to 3 months in the freezer.

ખજુર આમલી ની ચટણી – *Khajur amli ni chutni*

Date and tamarind chutney

This chutney recipe brings together the sweet flavour of dates and the tanginess of tamarind. More liquid than other chutneys, we like to dip all sorts of fritters, samosas and parathas in it.

Makes 1 jar
Preparation time: 10 mins
Soaking time: 1 hr
Cooking time: 25 mins

125 g dates, pitted
40 g jaggery
1 tbsp neutral cooking oil
½ tsp cumin seeds
1 tsp white sesame seeds
3 cm cassia bark
7 tbsp tamarind pulp
½ tsp ground ginger
½ tsp ground cumin
¼ tsp chilli powder (optional)
½ tsp salt

Cut the dates in half. Cover with 250 ml of water, leave to soak for 1 hour, then cook over low heat in the soaking water for 10 minutes.

Dissolve the jaggery in 60 ml of water over low heat, stirring occasionally. Remove from the heat as soon as the jaggery has dissolved (about 5 minutes).

In a saucepan, heat the oil over medium heat and fry the whole spices (seeds and cassia) for 1 minute.

Add the tamarind pulp, dissolved jaggery, ground spices and salt. Mix well before adding the dates and their cooking water. Leave to simmer for 10 minutes or until the chutney coats the back of the spoon.

Remove the cassia and leave to cool, off the hob.

When the mixture has cooled, whiz it in a blender, adjusting the salt and chilli to taste.

Tip

Store this chutney in an airtight jar in the fridge for up to 2–3 weeks.

Garlic paste, ginger paste and chilli paste

Garlic, ginger and chilli are an essential trio in our cooking, so rather than peel a clove of garlic, grate some ginger and chop a chilli for each recipe, I prefer to prepare each of them in the form of pastes that I freeze in large quantities so that I have enough on hand for a few weeks or months. Frozen in 1 teaspoon portions in ice-cube trays and taken out of the freezer as and when needed, these cubes of frozen paste can be put straight into hot oil along with the spices, or defrosted in the fridge 12 hours before needed.

પીસેલુ લસણ – *Pisselou lassan*

Garlic paste

Makes 20 tsp
Preparation time: 10 mins

150 g garlic (peeled)
1 tsp neutral oil (optional)
¼ tsp black salt (optional)

Whiz the peeled garlic cloves in a small food processor or with a hand-held blender until smooth. If necessary, add oil and salt.

Put teaspoons of the paste into an ice-cube tray and freeze.

પીસેલુ આદુ – *Pisselou adou*

Ginger paste

Makes 16 tsp
Preparation time: 10 mins

100 g fresh ginger
1 tsp neutral oil (optional)
⅛ tsp black salt (optional)

Peel the ginger, or not, if you prefer. If you prefer to keep the skin on, wash it thoroughly and wait until it is completely dry before moving on to the next step.

Grate the ginger using a fine grater or slice it and whiz it in a small food processor to a smooth paste (it won't be as smooth as the garlic paste, but that's normal). Add oil and salt if necessary.

Put teaspoons of the paste into an ice-cube tray and freeze.

પસિલા મર્ચા – *Pissela mircha*

Chilli paste

Makes 25 tsp
Preparation time: 10 mins

150 g your choice of green or red chillies (see p.16 for tips)

1 tsp neutral oil (optional)

¼ tsp black salt (optional)

If the chillies are hot, put on gloves before washing and drying them, and removing the stems.

Put the chillies (whole or cut into pieces depending on their size) in a small food processor and whiz to a smooth paste (it won't be as smooth as the garlic paste, but that's normal). Add oil and salt if necessary.

Put teaspoons of the paste into an ice-cube tray and freeze.

Tips

– As long as you mix in a little oil and salt, these pastes can be kept for a few days in the fridge in an airtight container.

– They can be kept in the freezer for up to 3 months. After about 24 hours, and once the pastes have frozen, you can put them in separate airtight jars.

તંદૂરી પેસ્ટ – *Tandoori paste*

Tandoori paste

Tandoori paste and tandoori masala are spice blends traditionally used to cook food in a tandoor. Made with toasted spices, garlic and fresh ginger, tandoori paste can be used on its own or mixed with yoghurt, garlic and fresh ginger to coat tofu (see p. 76) or vegetables such as cauliflower and potatoes before roasting in the oven or grilling on a barbecue.

Makes 90 g
Preparation time: 15 mins
Cooking time: 10 mins
Resting time: 15 mins

- 5 g fresh ginger
- 5 g garlic
- 2 tsp dried fenugreek leaves
- 2 tsp hot paprika
- 1 tsp sweet paprika
- ½ tsp grated nutmeg
- ¼ tsp ground turmeric
- 30 ml neutral oil
- 20 g tomato paste
- 1 tsp lemon juice
- 2 tsp maple syrup
- ½ tsp salt

For the whole spices:

- 2 tsp coriander seeds
- 1 tsp cumin seeds
- ½ tsp black peppercorns
- ½ tsp cloves
- 1 g cassia bark
- 5 green cardamom pods (pods and seeds separated)
- 1 small black cardamom pod (pod and seeds separated)

Peel the ginger and garlic.

Spread the whole spices out in a large non-stick frying pan and toast over low heat for 10 minutes or until they brown slightly and become fragrant. Stir regularly to make sure they don't burn.

Spread the toasted spices on a large plate and leave to cool completely before grinding them in an electric spice mill.

Whiz all the ingredients together to a smooth paste.

Tips

- To save time, you can make this paste from a ready-to-use mix. In that case, replace the whole spices and ground spices with 3 tablespoons of tandoori spices.
- This paste will keep for a few days in the fridge in an airtight container or in the freezer for up to 3 months.

સેકેલા જીરાનો ભૂકો – *Sekela jira no bhouko*

Toasted cumin powder

As with all spices, the flavour of cumin varies somewhat depending on how it is prepared: toasted, infused in oil, whole, coarsely crushed or finely ground. Toasting cumin accentuates its earthy, slightly smoky notes and enhances its nutty flavour. It's great in raita (see p. 142), dried fruit pickles (see p. 162) or in a paratha stuffing (see p. 136), but it's so delicious that we actually use it in all our recipes that call for ground cumin. Once you've tasted it, you'll most likely do the same.

Makes 50 g (about 25 tsp)
Preparation time: 5 mins
Cooking time: 2–3 mins
Resting time: 15 mins

50 g cumin seeds

Heat a large non-stick frying pan over medium-low heat and toast the cumin seeds, stirring regularly, for 2–3 minutes or until the seeds start to brown and to smoke a little. Just be careful they don't burn.

Immediately remove the pan from the heat and spread the toasted cumin seeds on a plate.

Leave to cool completely (about 15 minutes), then grind to a powder using an electric spice mill.

Tip

Store in an airtight, opaque jar, away from light, heat and moisture for up to 6 months. Beyond that, it will still be edible but its fragrance will begin to fade.

ગરમ મસાલા – *Garam masala*

Garam masala

Garam masala is a blend of spices generally added at the end of cooking to enhance the flavour of a dish. Although we speak of this condiment in the singular, there are in fact as many garam masalas as there are cooks, and each uses substantially different ingredients in varying quantities. However, each recipe includes a dominant number of hot spices – *garam* means 'hot' in both Hindi and Gujarati – such as cumin, black pepper, cloves, etc. My recipe is inspired by one that my mother's Pakistani friend Shazia makes.

Makes 75 g
Preparation time: 5 mins
Cooking time: 5 mins
Resting time: 15 mins

25 g coriander seeds
20 g cumin seeds
15 g peppercorns
10 g cloves
15 green cardamom pods (pods and seeds separated, about 2.5 g)
3 black cardamom pods (pods and seeds separated, about 2.5 g)
½ stick cinnamon (about 2.5 g)
3 x star anise
¼ tsp freshly grated nutmeg

Spread all the spices in a large non-stick frying pan and toast over low heat for 10 minutes or until they change colour and become fragrant. Stir regularly and be careful not to burn them.

Spread the toasted spices on a large plate and leave to cool completely before grinding them in an electric spice mill.

Tip

Store in an airtight, opaque jar, away from light, heat and moisture for up to 6 months. Beyond that, the masala will still be edible but its fragrance will begin to fade.

મીઠો ઇચાર – *Mitho itchar*

Dried fruit pickles

Although I don't have a sweet tooth, I have to admit that I really enjoy serving my Indian dishes with a syrupy chutney or pickles that add a nice balance to all the flavours, so this dried fruit pickle is one of the condiments I always make sure I have at home. For a long time, I made do with sweet commercial chutneys, but felt that I was eating a jam that was far too smooth and sweet, and with no particular flavour. Now, thanks to my mother's good advice, I've learnt how to make sweet pickles the way I like them, with lots of little pieces of dried fruit infused with spices.

Makes 1 large jar
Soaking time: 8 hrs
Preparation time: 10 mins
Cooking time: 30 mins

50 g dried figs
50 g dates, pitted
50 g dried apricots, chopped
25 g raisins
25 g dried cranberries
5 g fresh ginger
50 ml white wine vinegar
160 g white sugar
4 cloves
2 Ceylon cinnamon sticks
4 green cardamom pods
½ tsp chilli flakes (optional)
50 g raw cashew nuts
4 tsp tamarind pulp
⅛ tsp toasted, ground cumin
⅛ tsp salt

Soak the dried fruit in plenty of cold water for 8 hours. Drain, but keep the soaking water. Measure the soaking water. You will need 300 ml, so top it up with more water if necessary.

Cut the figs, dates and apricots into 1-cm pieces. Peel and chop the ginger.

In a sauté pan or saucepan, pour in the 300 ml of soaking water and the white vinegar, and add the sugar, whole spices and ginger. Stir and cook over medium heat for around 20 minutes or until the liquid starts to boil and becomes syrupy.

Add all the dried fruit, cashew nuts, tamarind, toasted cumin and salt, and cook for a further 10 minutes over medium heat.

Leave to cool before transferring the pickle to an airtight jar and storing in the fridge.

Tip

This pickle will keep for several weeks in an airtight container in the fridge.

ગાજર નો ઇચાર – *Gajar no itchar*

Vegetable pickles

This is a condiment that I particularly like for the touch of colour and crunch it adds to the dishes it accompanies. Try it with fritters, samosas, rice with vegetables and with lentils, spiced scrambled tofu and parathas.

Makes 4 jars
Preparation time: 30 mins
Cooking time: 3 mins
Fermentation time: 5 hrs

200 g carrots
100 g white cabbage
90 g green beans
70 g red pepper
50 g green pepper
10 g fresh ginger
8 tbsp neutral cooking oil
10 curry leaves
1 tsp black mustard seeds
1 tsp coriander seeds
4 tsp ground coriander
1 tsp ground turmeric
½ tsp chilli flakes
1 tsp toasted sesame seeds
½ tsp garlic paste
1 tsp salt
¼ tsp sugar
1 tbsp lemon juice
2 tbsp white vinegar

Peel and grate the carrots. Chop the cabbage. Top and tail the green beans and cut into 2-cm pieces. Seed and finely chop the peppers. Peel and finely chop the ginger. Put all the vegetables into a large bowl.

Add the ground coriander, ground turmeric, chilli flakes, toasted sesame seeds, garlic paste, salt and sugar to the vegetables. Mix well, cover the bowl and leave to stand for 30 minutes.

Heat the oil in a non-stick frying pan over medium-low heat and fry the whole spices (curry leaves and seeds) for 3 minutes, then pour the hot spiced oil over the vegetables. Stir to ensure that all the vegetables are thoroughly coated.

Add the lemon juice and vinegar, mix well, cover and leave to ferment for 5 hours at room temperature before transferring the pickle to jars.

Tip

Store in an airtight jar for up to 2 weeks in the fridge or up to 3 months in the freezer.

બરિસ્ટો – *Biristo*

Fried onions

Fried onions add a caramelised note to all kinds of dishes and are particularly popular sprinkled over plain or spiced rice, biryani or rice with vegetables as well as vegetables with lentils. They can be mixed into the rice at the beginning of cooking or added just before serving.

Serves 4
Preparation time: 10 mins
Cooking time: 15 mins

500 g yellow onions
frying oil (see p. 32 for tips)

Peel and thinly slice the onions.

In a saucepan or frying pan, heat 1 cm of oil over medium-high heat. When the oil is hot, add the onions.

As soon as they start to brown, stir constantly.

Once the onions are golden brown, remove them with a skimmer and place on a plate lined with kitchen paper.

Tip

Store the fried onions in an airtight jar, at room temperature, for up to 3 months.

Desserts

ગાજર નો હલવો – *Gajar no halvo*

Silky carrots with vanilla

Thanks to their naturally sweet flavour and high water content, carrots can be used in all kinds of desserts: cakes, custards and sorbets. In India, they are the star ingredient of *gajar no halvo*, a warm, melt-in-the-mouth dessert made with grated carrots cooked in sweetened vanilla milk. At last, a real dessert that's made with a lot of vegetables!

Serves 5
Preparation time: 10 mins
Cooking time: 30 mins

500 g carrots

400 ml soya milk or full-fat plant-based milk (see p. 25 for tips)

¼ tsp vanilla powder or ¼ split vanilla pod

100 g white sugar

3 tbsp plant-based margarine

2 tsp ground almonds

Peel and grate the carrots.

Mix the grated carrots, 100 ml of water and the soya milk in a saucepan and heat over medium-high heat.

When the mixture starts to boil, add the vanilla, sugar and margarine.

Continue cooking over medium heat until all the liquid has been absorbed.

Serve warm, sprinkled with ground almonds.

અનનસ નો હલવો – *Pineapple no halvo*

Crushed pineapple with cream and cardamom

Here's a fruity, creamy and comforting dessert that can be served either warm or cold, and which, like many spiced dishes, is best prepared the day before. In this case, it's to give the pineapple enough time to absorb the flavours of the cardamom and saffron.

Serves 5
Infusing time: 2 hrs
Preparation time: 10 mins
Cooking time: 30 mins

4 saffron strands

400 g pineapple pieces in syrup (drained weight)

50 g plant-based margarine

½ tsp cardamom seeds

1 tsp ground almonds

2 tbsp sugar

100 ml soya cream

For serving:

chopped pistachios and/or little chunks of pineapple

Infuse the saffron strands in 1 tablespoon of hot water for 2 hours.

Drain the pineapple chunks, then mash them with a fork or a potato masher.

Melt the margarine in a saucepan over low heat, add the cardamom seeds and fry for 2 minutes. Add the pineapple and cook over medium heat, stirring regularly, for around 15 minutes or until the mixture thickens and coats the back of the spoon.

Stir in the ground almonds, sugar and soya cream. Continue cooking over low heat, stirring regularly, for around 10 minutes or until the cream has been absorbed.

Lastly, pour in the saffron-infused water and stir well. Serve warm or cold, sprinkled with the chopped pistachios and/or little chunks of pineapple.

બટેટા નો હલવો – *Batata no halvo*

Creamy potatoes with cardamom

While it's perhaps not so surprising to find vegetables such as carrots, courgettes or beetroot in a dessert, it's certainly more unusual to come across potatoes! *Batata no halvo* combines the comforting and filling qualities of mashed potatoes with sugar and cardamom. As with a risotto, *batata no halvo* requires almost continuous stirring, but when you love potatoes, what's a little extra work?

Serves 8
Preparation time: 10 mins
Cooking time: 1 hr

400 g potatoes (any variety used for potato salad, or for steaming or sautéeing)
70 g plant-based margarine (at least 80% fat content)
¼ tsp ground cardamom
90 g white sugar
1 tbsp ground almonds

For serving:
almonds and/or pistachios, chopped
soya cream (optional)

Steam the potatoes for around 20 minutes, then peel them. Mash while still warm.

In a saucepan, melt the margarine over medium heat and add the mashed potatoes and cardamom, stirring for 20 minutes.

Add the sugar and stir for 10 minutes. Add the ground almonds and stir for a further 10 minutes.

Leave to cool and serve the *halvo* sprinkled with the chopped almonds and/or pistachios, and with a drizzle of plant-based cream if you wish.

ફિરની – *Firni*

Creamy rice with saffron and cardamom

***Firni* is one of my favourite Indian desserts, but my mother never used to make it. So it was usually at my Auntie Banou's house that I enjoyed it, and it was at her side where I learned to make it. This cardamom- and saffron-scented cream needs to be chilled for some hours before serving for the desired thickness and temperature to be reached.**

Serves 4
Infusing time: 2 hrs
Preparation time: 10 mins
Cooking time: 40 mins
Chilling time: 12 hrs

4 saffron strands
60 g semi-wholegrain rice flour
375 ml soya or oat milk
¼ tsp ground cardamom
60 g white sugar

For decorating:
ground almonds
flaked almonds

Infuse the saffron strands in 1 tablespoon of hot water 2 hours in advance.

In a bowl, whisk the rice flour and 175 ml of the plant-based milk to a smooth and lump-free mixture.

In a saucepan, mix the remaining milk, 250 ml water and the cardamom over medium heat until it comes to the first boil, about 8 minutes.

Pour in the milk and rice flour mixture, then add the sugar and whisk well. Continue cooking, whisking regularly for 15–30 minutes, until the mixture thickens (it will thicken faster if you use oat milk).

Remove from the heat, add the infused saffron and mix well.

Divide the cream between four individual ramekins and leave to cool before covering and leaving in the fridge for at least 12 hours.

Before serving, sprinkle with ground almonds and/or flaked almonds.

ખીર – *Khir*

Rice pudding with cardamom and saffron

Khir **is a bit like rice pudding, but with a little extra spice and dried fruit. In India,** ***khir*** **is often served with piping hot puris (see p. 138), which are used to scoop up every last bite. This combination may seem surprising at first, but these fried breads are the perfect accompaniment to this creamy dessert.**

Serves 4–6
Soaking time: 2 hrs
Preparation time: 10 mins
Cooking time: 1 hr 15 mins
Chilling time: 24 hrs

- 3 saffron strands
- 45 g basmati rice
- 10 g raisins
- 40 g white sugar + ¼ tsp for the raisins
- 700 ml creamy plant-based milk
- ⅛ tsp ground cardamom
- 1 tsp ground almonds
- 1 tbsp almonds and/or pistachios, chopped

For decoration:

- ground almonds
- slivered almonds and/or pistachios

Before starting to prepare the *khir*, infuse the saffron strands for 2 hours in 1 tablespoon of hot water. Pour in enough cold water to cover the rice, and enough boiling water to cover the raisins plus the ¼ tsp of sugar. Leave to soak for 1 hour.

Pour 2 cm of water into the bottom of a large saucepan and heat over medium-high heat for 3 minutes (this step will prevent the milk from sticking to the bottom of the pan). Pour out the water (reuse it for something else). Pour the milk into the saucepan and bring to the boil over medium-high heat, stirring regularly.

Drain the rice, coarsely crush the grains between your fingers and add to the boiling milk. Cook the rice over medium-low heat for 40 minutes. Stir every 5 minutes to prevent the milk from curdling.

Stir in the sugar, cardamom, ground almonds, chopped almonds and/or pistachios and the drained raisins, and continue cooking over medium heat for 30 minutes or until the grains of rice are visible on the surface.

There should still be a little liquid, but this will be largely absorbed as the mixture cools.

Remove from the heat and stir in the saffron-infused water.

Divide the *khir* between individual ramekins or pour it into a large bowl. Leave to cool, then put it in the fridge for at least 24 hours to allow this creamy dessert to firm up.

Sprinkle with ground almonds, slivered almonds and/or pistachios and serve cold.

Tip

Although regular soya milk is usually a good substitute for animal milk, it does not produce the same creamy texture as the traditional *khir* recipe. I recommend using a full-fat plant-based milk that is as creamy as animal milk: these include brands like Oatly®, Alpro®'s creamy plant-based milks or a mixture of oat and cashew milk (30/70). However, no matter which plant-based milk you choose, make sure that it does not contain added sugar.

ગુલાબ ઈલાયચી ફાલુદો – *Goulab elaichi faloudo*

Rose and cardamom flan

This flan is one of the desserts I most often make when we have guests for dinner. Not only is it quick to prepare, even if you make a large quantity, it's also light enough to enjoy after a hearty meal. It's so full of flavour that you'll forget how simple it is!

Serves 4
Preparation time: 10 mins
Cooking time: 15 mins
Chilling time: 6 hrs

400 ml soya milk
100 ml soya cream
60 g white sugar
½ tsp cardamom seeds
½ tsp agar-agar
1 tsp ground almonds
4 tsp rosewater

For decorating:
ground almonds or pistachios

Put all the ingredients into a saucepan and heat over medium heat, stirring until the mixture starts to boil, then reduce the heat to medium-low and continue cooking for 1 minute.

Pour the mixture into four individual ramekins, taking care to remove the cardamom seeds (they usually sink to the bottom of the pan).

Decorate with ground almonds or pistachios, leave to cool, then leave the ramekins in the fridge for at least 6 hours. Enjoy!

મીઠી સેવ – *Mithi sev*

Toasted vermicelli with raisins

These grilled vermicelli, made from wheat flour and resembling Italian angel hair pasta, should not be confused with the fried vermicelli made from chickpea flour in the recipe for tomato *shaak* with fried vermicelli (see p. 45). In India, this long, thin pasta is eaten in sweet dishes rather than savoury ones.

Serves 5
Soaking time: 1 hr
Preparation time: 10 mins
Cooking time: 25 mins
Resting time: 5 mins

- 30 g raisins
- 4 tbsp white sugar + 1 tsp for the raisins
- 25 g plant-based margarine
- 100 g toasted wheat vermicelli (see p. 27 for tips)
- ⅓ vanilla pod

For serving:
flaked almonds

Cover the raisins with boiling water, add the teaspoon of white sugar and leave to soak for 1 hour.

Melt the margarine in a saucepan over low heat, then add the roughly broken vermicelli and the split vanilla pod. Stir regularly until the vermicelli turn golden brown, about 5–10 minutes.

Lift the lid and quickly pour in 160 ml of boiling water, then cover immediately to prevent splattering.

After 3 minutes, take off the lid, stir in the sugar, raisins and 160 ml of boiling water and cook, covered, for a further 20 minutes, stirring from time to time.

Remove the pan from the heat and leave to rest, covered, for 5 minutes.

Serve warm, sprinkled with flaked almonds.

સીરખુરરમો – *Sirkhourmo*

Vermicelli with milk and vanilla

***Sirkhourmo* is a bit like rice pudding, but made with pasta instead of rice. It can be eaten warm or cold, but I prefer the latter as it becomes a little denser and creamier after a few hours in the fridge.**

Serves 4
Soaking time: 1 hr
Preparation time: 10 mins
Cooking time: 35 mins

- 30 g raisins
- 60 g white sugar + 1 tsp for the raisins
- 10 g plant-based margarine + ½ tsp
- 50 g toasted wheat vermicelli (see p. 27 for tips)
- ¼ vanilla pod
- 500 ml full-fat plant-based milk (see p. 25 for tips)
- 1 tbsp ground almonds

For serving:

slivered almonds and/or pistachios

Cover the raisins with boiling water, add the teaspoon of white sugar and leave to soak for 1 hour.

Melt the 10 g of margarine in a saucepan over low heat, then add the roughly broken vermicelli and the split vanilla pod. Stir regularly until the vermicelli turn golden brown, about 5–10 minutes.

Melt the ½ teaspoon of margarine in a small frying pan over medium heat and fry the drained raisins for a few minutes to plump them up.

Add the raisins to the vermicelli and fry for 2 minutes. Pour in 125 ml of boiling water and the plant-based milk, add the sugar and leave to cook over medium-low heat for 15 minutes.

As soon as the mixture starts to boil, turn the heat to low and stir in the ground almonds. Continue cooking for 5 minutes, stirring regularly to prevent the milk from curdling.

Divide the mixture into 4 ramekins. Leave to cool, then top with slivered almonds and/or pistachios. Serve immediately or chill in the fridge and serve cold.

કેળા ના ભજ્યા – *Kera na bhajyia*

Banana fritters

This quick and easy recipe for banana slices in a cardamom-scented batter is a delicious treat with a caramelised flavour that melts in your mouth. However, I should warn you about the main problem with this recipe: making sure you don't eat all the fritters as they are fried!

Makes 20 fritters
Preparation time: 10 mins
Cooking time: 10 mins

2 medium bananas
85 g T45 wheat flour
⅛ tsp ground cardamom
⅛ tsp baking powder
50 ml soya milk
oil for frying
icing sugar

Peel and cut the bananas into 1.5-cm thick slices.

In a separate bowl, combine the flour, ground cardamom and baking powder.

Mix 50 ml of water with the soya milk. Gradually whisk into the dry ingredients, whisking to a smooth and lump-free batter Add the banana slices.

Prepare a fryer (see p. 32 for tips) with about 3 cm of oil.

Using a large spoon, take each banana slice, generously coated in the batter, and drop it gently into the hot oil. Fry several fritters at a time, spacing them about 2 cm apart, for 2 minutes on each side until golden brown.

Place the fritters on a plate lined with kitchen paper, dust with icing sugar and enjoy immediately.

નાનખતાય – *Nankhatai*

Cardamom shortbread

These delicious cardamom-scented shortbreads delighted me not only when I was a child, but continue to do so now as well. Every time I stayed with my family for the holidays, I'd leave with a box full of *nankhatais*, and my relatives would always bring me some when they came to visit. For this plant-based version, I've simply replaced the traditional butter and ghee with a high-fat margarine to create an equally delicious alternative.

Makes 25 shortbreads
Preparation time: 15 mins
Baking time: 25 mins

- 200 g high-fat plant-based margarine (block form, at least 75% fat)
- 100 g icing sugar
- 300 g T45 white wheat flour
- 50 g cornflour
- ½ tsp ground cardamom
- 1 pinch salt
- whole almonds or pistachios for decorating (optional)

Using an electric mixer, a food processor fitted with an S-blade or a hand whisk (and lots of elbow grease!), beat the chopped margarine and icing sugar together until smooth and lump-free.

Sift the flour and cornflour together. Stir in the ground cardamom and the pinch of salt. Using a flexible spatula, gradually stir the dry ingredients into the beaten margarine. When the mixture becomes too hard to stir, use your hands to mix the dough until you have a smooth, lump-free ball.

Preheat the oven to 200°C/180°C fan/gas mark 6. Take about 25 g of the dough, shape it into a ball and flatten it out to form a round disc about 1 cm thick. Using a round-tipped knife, lightly press four times into the top of each disc, or simply make a cross in the centre. Place 1 almond or 1 pistachio in the middle.

Put the shortbreads on a baking tray lined with parchment paper as you go, then bake in the oven for around 25 minutes. The shortbreads should be nice and golden.

Leave to cool completely and firm up on a wire rack before serving.

Drinks

મસાલા ચા – *masala chai*

Spiced tea

An emblematic Indian beverage, the masala chai – literally 'spiced tea' – found on the menus of Western cafés is a world away from chai as we know it in India. Traditionally, water, milk and spices are boiled together for several minutes to produce a smooth drink with varying degrees of spiciness, depending on individual tastes.

Makes 1 cup
Cooking time: 10 mins

1 green cardamom pod or 1 cm piece vanilla pod

125 ml creamy or barista plant-based oat milk (see p. 25 for tips)

1 tsp Assam black tea

1 tsp white sugar

5 mm cassia bark

1 clove

Split or crush the cardamom or the vanilla pod.

Put all the ingredients in a small saucepan with 125 ml of water, stir and bring to the boil over medium heat.

As soon as the mixture comes to the boil, reduce the heat and continue simmering for 5 minutes.

Strain, serve and enjoy.

Tips

- You can also make masala chai without milk.
- This tea can be prepared with other spices such as ginger (fresh or dried) and star anise.
- Each region in India has a different version of this tea.
- The amber-coloured, intensely flavoured Assam tea from north-eastern India is particularly suited to a milky version.

હરિરો – *Hariro*

Hot milk with almond and saffron

A comforting drink par excellence, *hariro* is something my mother used to prepare for me when I wasn't feeling well. I still make it on winter evenings when I need something both warm and sweet. Made with ground almonds, which gives it a unique and delicious texture, and flavoured with saffron and cardamom, this hot milk drink is almost like a dessert!

Makes 1 mug
Cooking time: 13 mins

10 g plant-based margarine
2 tsp ground almonds
250 ml creamy or barista plant-based oat milk (see p. 25 for tips)
1 tsp white sugar
2 saffron strands
1 large pinch ground cardamom

Heat the margarine in a small saucepan over low heat.

Add the ground almonds and fry until golden brown and fragrant (about 2 minutes).

Add the milk, sugar, saffron and cardamom and cook over low heat for 10 minutes, stirring regularly.

Enjoy piping hot.

Tip

As explained on p. 18, saffron is best infused in water for at least 1 hour before being used. If you have time to prepare this drink in advance, we recommend infusing 1 saffron strand (not 2) in 1 tablespoon of hot water for 1 hour and adding the infused water to the milk, just before you heat it.

ગુલાબ અને તકમરયા નુ દૂધ – *Goulab ane tukmaria nou doudh*

Milk with rose syrup and basil seeds

An aromatic plant native to Central Africa and South East Asia, basil is not widely used in Indian cuisine. However, the seeds, known as *tukmaria* or *sabja*, are widely used in Ayurveda (traditional Indian medicine) and in *faloodas*, dessert drinks of which there are various kinds across both India and South East Asia. These mucilaginous seeds swell and become gelatinous when soaked in water. High in fibre, protein and minerals, they are valued for their texture and refreshing flavour.

Makes 2 glasses
Soaking time: 30 mins
Preparation time: 5 mins

½ tsp basil seeds (*Ocimum basilicum*)

2 tbsp rose syrup (or more or less, to taste)

400 ml very cold plant-based milk (see p. 25 for tips)

Put the basil seeds into a small bowl, cover completely with water and leave to swell in the fridge for 30 minutes.

Pour 1 tablespoon of rose syrup into each glass. Pour half of the milk to each glass and half of the swollen basil seeds, mix well and enjoy.

Tips

- This drink is best enjoyed chilled, so try to prepare it in advance and leave it in the fridge for a few hours.
- As they soak in the water the seeds tend to stick to each other. If this happens, add a little water, then stir to separate the seeds. The soaked seeds can be kept for 24–48 hours in the fridge.
- As not all varieties of basil have the same mucilaginous properties, we suggest you buy seeds labelled *tukmaria* or *sabja*, that are available in Indian grocery shops or online.

લસ્સી – *Lassi*

Lassi

A cool, sweet yoghurt-based drink, lassi can be enjoyed at any time of day and is generally served at festive meals. Here is not one, but five recipes with different floral, fruity or spicy flavours.

Plain lassi

Makes 2 glasses
Preparation time: 5 mins
Chilling time: 1 hr

250 g soya yoghurt
20 g white sugar

Using a whisk or an immersion blender fitted with an emulsifying blade (4 blades), whisk or whiz the yoghurt and sugar until smooth.

Pour in 100 ml of water and continue whisking or whizzing until the mixture is frothy.

Refrigerate for at least 1 hour, then whisk or whiz again before serving.

Rose lassi

Makes 2 glasses
Preparation time: 5 mins
Chilling time: 1 hr

250 g soya yoghurt
20 g white sugar (omit when using rose syrup)
rose flavour: 2 drops rose essence OR 2 tsp rosewater OR rose syrup

Using a whisk or an immersion blender fitted with an emulsifying blade (4 blades), whisk or whiz the yoghurt and sugar until smooth.

Pour in 100 ml of water (reduce to 90 ml if using rosewater) and the rose-flavoured ingredient of your choice and continue whisking or whizzing until frothy.

Refrigerate for at least 1 hour, then whisk or whiz again before serving.

Cardamom lassi

Makes 2 glasses
Preparation time: 5 mins
Chilling time: 1 hr

250 g soya yoghurt

20 g white sugar

⅛ tsp ground cardamom

Using a whisk or an immersion blender fitted with an emulsifying blade (4 blades), whisk or whiz the yoghurt and sugar until smooth.

Add 100 ml of water and the ground cardamom and continue whisking or whizzing until the mixture is frothy.

Refrigerate for at least 1 hour, then whisk or whiz again before serving.

Saffron lassi

Makes 2 glasses
Preparation time: 5 mins
Chilling time: 1 hr

2 saffron strands

250 g soya yoghurt

20 g white sugar

Place the saffron strands in 1 tablespoon of hot water and leave to stand for 1 hour.

Using a whisk or an immersion blender fitted with an emulsifying blade (4 blades), whisk or whiz the yoghurt and sugar until smooth.

Add 85 ml of water and the saffron-flavoured water and continue whisking or whizzing until the mixture is frothy.

Refrigerate for at least 1 hour, then whisk or whiz again before serving.

Mango lassi

Makes 2 glasses
Preparation time: 5 mins
Chilling time: 1 hr

125 g soya yoghurt

125 g Alphonso mango pulp or fresh mango pulp

⅛ tsp ground cardamom

Using a whisk or an immersion blender fitted with an emulsifying blade (4 blades), whisk or whiz the yoghurt and mango until smooth.

Add 100 ml of water and the ground cardamom and continue whisking or whizzing until the mixture is frothy. Adjust the amount of water until you have the right consistency.

Refrigerate for at least 1 hour, then whisk or whiz again before serving.

કેસર એલાયચી શરબત – *Kessar elaichi sharbat*

Saffron and cardamom syrup

Kessar elaichi sharbat **is a syrup deliciously flavoured with saffron and cardamom usually enjoyed on festive occasions such as weddings or religious celebrations. It's served in small quantities in shot glasses, but I like it so much that I always end up having several.**

Makes 200 ml of syrup (for about 15 glasses)
Preparation time: 5 mins
Cooking time: 10 mins
Resting time: 2 hrs

3 green cardamom pods
100 g white sugar
6 saffron strands

For decorating:
slivered almonds and pistachios

Crush or split the cardamom pods.

In a small saucepan, bring 100 ml of water and the cardamom to the boil over medium-high heat.

As soon as the water boils, add the sugar and mix well until it has completely dissolved, then continue cooking over low heat, covered, for 5 minutes.

Remove from the heat, stir in the saffron and leave to stand for at least 2 hours before removing the spices and transferring the cooled syrup to a small bottle or airtight sealed jar. Store in the fridge.

Just before serving, mix 1–2 tablespoons of syrup with 200 ml of cold water, top with slivered almonds and pistachios and enjoy.

Tip

This syrup will keep for up to 2 weeks in the fridge, in an airtight container.

મસાલા છાશ – *masala tchaas*

Savoury yoghurt drink

Masala *tchaas* is a savoury drink similar to lassi, but spicier and less creamy. We like to drink it during a meal or at the end of it. I particularly enjoy it with spicy dishes as yoghurt has a cooling effect and a few sips of *tchaas* soothes any burning sensations in the mouth and throat.

Makes 2 glasses
Preparation time: 5 mins
Chilling time: 1 hr

200 g soya yoghurt
⅛ tsp toasted, ground cumin
⅛ tsp freshly ground black pepper
2 pinches black salt (*kala namak*) or fine salt

Using a whisk or an immersion blender fitted with an emulsifying blade (4 blades), whisk or whiz all the ingredients with 100 ml of water until smooth.

Refrigerate for at least 1 hour, then whisk or whiz again before serving.

Tips

- You can serve each glass with a pinch of ground cumin and pepper and a generous pinch of finely chopped mint and/or coriander leaves.
- Substitute the ground cumin and pepper with *chaat* masala, a blend of spices generally including dried mango powder, asafoetida, cumin, coriander seeds, chilli, ginger, black salt and pepper. Usually used to spice up typical street food snacks (*chaat*) all over India, *chaat* masala is also very popular in *tchaas*.

Appendices

Table of recipes

Condiments 140

Desserts............................... 168

Drinks 192

Index of recipes

R

S

T

V

W

Y

Index of ingredients

Tomato

Tomato paste

Tomato sauce

Toor dal (pigeon peas)

Vanilla pods

Vermicelli, fried

Vermicelli, toasted wheat

White cabbage

White sesame seeds

Yellow onions

Menu ideas

If you'd like a few ideas for designing some menus using our recipes, here are a few suggestions, based on the season and the occasion.

Spring menu

Lentil fritters (p. 108) and date and tamarind chutney (p. 151)

•

Pea *shaak* with coconut milk (p. 38), spiced rice (p. 88) and dried fruit pickles (p. 162)

•

Silky carrots with vanilla (p. 170)

Summer menu

Grilled aubergine mash (p. 50)

•

Scrambled tofu with spices (p. 78)

•

Naans or *laccha* parathas (p. 129 or 131)
Vegetable pickles (p. 165)

•

Creamy rice with saffron and cardamom (p. 177)

Autumn menu

Yoghurt and chickpea-flour soup (p. 82)

•

Spinach and potato *shaak* (p. 42) and chapatis or puris (p. 126 or 138)

•

Vegetable pickles (p. 165) or dried fruit pickles (p. 162)

•

Toasted vermicelli with raisins (p. 185)

Winter menu

Cauliflower *shaak* (p. 54) and your choice of dal (pp. 62 to 68)

•

Basmati rice with coconut milk (p. 91)

•

Your choice of pickles (p. 162 or 165)

•

Vermicelli with milk and vanilla (p. 186)

Festive menu

Mung bean samosas (p. 121) and your choice of green chutney (p. 146 or 149)

•

Biryani (p. 100) and *kachumber* (p. 145)

•

Crushed pineapple
with cream and cardamom (p. 173)

•

Lassi and masala *tchaas* (p. 200 and 207)

Child-friendly menu

Potato fritters (p. 111)
and date and tamarind chutney (p. 151)

•

Rice with vegetables and coconut milk (p. 95)

•

Rose and cardamom
flan (p. 182)

Acknowledgements

To Marie Laforêt. You were the first to believe in this project, and we are honoured that our book will be part of this wonderful collection! Thank you for your trust in us.

We would like to thank the Solar team, and in particular Fanny and Diane, who have shaped our collection of personal recipes into such a magnificent book, taking care to include everything that was close to our hearts. Thank you for your attention to detail, for listening to us and for your sound advice throughout this adventure.

To Manon. We were deeply touched by your enthusiasm when you were photographing our dishes, and by your warmth and attentiveness during the photo shoots. You have captured our creations exactly as we wanted them to be.

Special thanks go to Dominique, who painstakingly re-read the first part of this book and provided invaluable advice on how to refine and clarify my writing. I can't thank you enough for all the support you've given me with my various writing projects over the years, despite the eight thousand or so kilometres between us.

Thanks also to Kevin, Shazia, Elie and Christine, who made their printers, scanners and computer skills available to us, making the final stages of writing our manuscript easier when my mother was in Grenoble and I was in Fribourg.

Thank you to the friends I regularly have the pleasure of welcoming to my table, and whose enthusiasm for my cooking gave me the confidence to write this book. Special thanks go to Ophélie and Éric, whose many compliments after every shared meal always move me; to Christian, Julia and Andreas, whose feedback on the initial recipes in this book encouraged us to continue.

I would also like to thank my friends and colleagues who followed this project from start to finish and whose support was invaluable as the deadline for our manuscript approached. Special thanks go to Elisenda, Lisa and Fikir, who always listen and brighten up my days at school.

And to friends who are far away, but whose support is no less valuable. I would especially like to thank Muelle and Natalia, who reassured and encouraged me when I needed it most, as well as Loetitia, whose support on the home stretch was much appreciated. Your interest in this book is incredibly heart-warming.

Thank you to the readers of my blog and my webzine, Cardamome & Curcuma, whose feedback on my writing and recipes enables me to continue pursuing a professional activity that contributes to my self-fulfilment. I would like to express my sincere gratitude to my Tippers, whose trust, generosity and support meant the world to me during challenging times.

I would like to thank my aunt, Banou Mami, and my cousins, Zehra, Ben and Ilmasse, for the delicious Indian dishes I have enjoyed since I was a child. My cooking is imbued – either directly or indirectly – with all that you have passed on to me during the countless meals we have shared together. I am particularly grateful for the care and love with which you adapted your recipes for me since I went vegan.

Thank you to my daughter, whose birth inspired me to start documenting our family recipes, and whose love of flatbreads and deep frying encouraged me to embrace new culinary challenges! For all you spice lovers out there, I'm thrilled to be able to share with you – through this book – some of the culinary knowledge that has been passed down through our family for generations.

A huge thanks to my husband, undoubtedly the biggest fan of my cooking! I still remember the first meal I cooked for you: butter chicken. My cooking has evolved considerably since then, becoming more aligned with my values, and it's with a rare enthusiasm and open-mindedness that you've embraced these changes. I am very grateful for your support throughout the creation of this book, and for organising for my mother and me to spend several weeks of our holiday in the kitchen, not to mention your dedication in testing and tasting each and every one of our dishes. It's a pleasure to cook for someone who is such a curious foodie.

Thank you to my mother, the best cook in the world! I've always loved your cooking, and I'm extremely indebted to you for the patience and love with which you passed on your culinary knowledge. I'm also grateful for the open-mindedness you showed when I went vegan. Thank you also for your unflagging encouragement and support, which have enabled me to achieve so much in my life, including writing this book. Your love carries me through every day.

Published in 2025 by
Grub Street
4 Rainham Close
London
SW11 6SS

Email: food@grubstreet.co.uk
Web: www.grubstreet.co.uk
X: @grub_street
Facebook: Grub Street Publishing
Instagram: grubstreetpublishinguk

ISBN: 978-1-911714-32-3
A CIP catalogue for this book is available from the British Library

Published originally in French as *Cuisine Indienne Vegan*

Photography: Manon Gouhier
Graphic Design: Julia Philipps
Layout: Joséphine Cormier

Printed and bound by Finidr